IN LOVING MEMORY

A Story of Love, Loss, and Living On

Diana Monique Soriano

ISBN 978-1-0980-9161-3 (paperback)
ISBN 978-1-0980-9162-0 (digital)

Christian Faith Publishing, Inc.
832 Park Avenue
Meadville, PA 16335
www.christianfaithpublishing.com

Printed in the United States of America

Dedication

For Bobby Justin Pagan, my soul mate and the love of my life. Thank you for showing me the meaning of true love. For loving me so deeply and giving me memories to cherish for a lifetime. I hope you're looking down on me smiling, and I hope I have made you proud. I love you, and I believe in my heart that one day I'll see you again when you greet me at the pearly gates. Until then, my guardian angel, I'll continue to keep your memory alive.

To Peggy Pagan (Mama), thank you for raising such a wonderful son. He loved and looked up to you so much! Thank you for embracing me and accepting me as your own. You will always be a second mother to me. I love you Mama.

To the Pagan family: Robert, Paula, Jodie, Angela, Ana, Chris, and Miguel, thank you for accepting me and treating me like another member of the family all these years. I love you guys so much. I hold you all near and dear to my heart because you are all that I have left of Bobby, and I can never give that up. Angela, I am so grateful for our relationship. I know Bobby is looking down on us smiling. I can't wait to be able to tell him "I told you they would love me! Also not once did your sisters beat me up!" Y'all will *always* be my family.

To Rundell Logan, my sister and best friend for life. You have no idea how much I cherish our friendship. You have been there for me through *every* up and down since 2008. You are the definition of a true friend, and I look forward to all our future endeavors sis. Thank you for encouraging me to get my story out. May God bless you always.

To Kortney Battles, thank you sis, for the wonderful memories that you helped me create with Bobby. We really had some of the best times together. Thank you for being there for me when he deployed, during his memorial ceremony, and to help me through mourning once I returned from deployment. I love you, and you are another sister for life!

To my 4th ID family: Thank you for giving me the opportunity to lay my fiancé to rest. It was a kind gesture that I will never forget. I was just a Private First Class, Bobby and I were not legally married, but you treated the situation as if we were and sent me home to bury him. I can't thank you enough and will always be grateful for that opportunity. 4th IBCT, 4th ID has a very special place in my heart and to this day has remained my favorite unit.

Finally, to my son, Cameron Isaiah Borja. I pray that one day you find a love of your own, one that I hope I get to witness. Until then, know that I love you with all my heart and soul. Don't you ever forget it. You are my reason for existence, and I love you beyond what words can ever express.

Contents

Preface

This book is my reflection on finding my soul mate at a young age and then losing him to the war in Afghanistan. It will depict the side of Bobby Justin Pagan that I got to experience. I will reflect on my experience of our deployment to Afghanistan. I will try to describe the pain of losing him when he was killed in action (KIA). I will discuss my healing process and provide a snippet of how my life has been since experiencing his loss. In this book, I will provide a reflection of our relationship, what I experienced when I was informed of his loss, and the raw emotions I felt. I will speak on my dysfunctional healing process and what it has been like trying to restore my life and live on. Lastly, I will describe the impact that Bobby had on my life. This book will depict some very painful memories but will also entail a beautiful love story that unfortunately had a tragic end. I knew I had a story to tell, but I wasn't ready to share it. I struggled writing this book because it forced me to go into a mental space that for years I have tried to block out. Not only that, I struggled with the thought that people may not take what I have to say seriously because I did not serve in a combat arms position. Some people discredit service, deployment experiences, and mental disorders such as PTSD when it derives from a person who served in a noncombat arms position. I know firsthand because one of my own family members has openly discredited my military service despite having served ten years.

Over time I have realized that we all have different roles in the military. We serve as different pieces to a puzzle. Without each specific piece, the puzzle cannot be whole. It would be lacking. While I may have been a "paper pusher" as they like to call me, that doesn't negate the fact that my military experience has traumatically affected me and has an impact in my life. I hope that by sharing my story, I can somehow shed light on how someone in a non-combat arms position can be affected by war.

While this book is not specifically on PTSD, I hope to get people to understand that PTSD can come from various traumatic events; it is not a cookie-cutter diagnosis. I also hope that I can somehow help others to come forward and speak out on their experiences in the military, whether good or bad. Last, I hope to somehow bring some sort of comfort to those who have lost loved ones who served in the military. I understand the impact the loss of a loved one has on your life, especially when they are killed in action. The circumstances may be different, but I understand the pain. I understand the feeling of despair, the feeling of hopelessness. I understand the emptiness you feel and the numbness that overcomes your body. I understand the feeling of loneliness despite how many people surround you. And what most people won't speak on, I understand the feeling of abandonment by a loved one you weren't ready to say goodbye to. I pray that this book somehow touches the heart of others, especially those who have experienced a loss like I have. There are no words that can ever make it better, but know that you are not alone.

Grab your tissues, I already have mine.

Introduction

I met Bobby when I was eighteen years old. He died three weeks after my twentieth birthday. Bobby was only twenty-three years old when he was Killed in Action out on the frontlines of Southern Afghanistan. To this day, I cherish our memories together along with the e-mails and letters we wrote to each other throughout our deployment. In those letters and e-mails, we both openly expressed our love for each other which went way deeper beyond any physical aspect. It was real. We laughed, we argued, we made up, and we loved each other immensely. Anyone who spent time with us can attest to the love and the bond that we shared with one another. He wanted to marry me, and even more so, he wanted me to be the mother of his children. I wanted nothing more than to be his wife, and I felt honored that he chose me as the person he wanted to have children with. I so badly wanted to be able to give him children, especially a son because he wanted a boy first, someone to carry on his name.

Unfortunately, I never had the chance to make his wish come true. Two weeks before we were scheduled to take leave from our year-long deployment in Afghanistan, Bobby was Killed in Action, and my life changed forever. I never felt so broken in my life. To this day, I still cry and often wonder, "Why Bobby?" The pain of losing Bobby still hurts my soul to the core. When I think back on the day that I lost him, and everything that has happened since, my heart breaks. That pain still lingers within the depths of my soul. I don't know how to suitably describe the pain, but I can describe what I physically experience. I cry uncontrollably. My ribs tremble. My chest gets tight. I feel a sharp pain in my heart. My throat feels like it is closed, and my airway feels blocked. I find it hard to breathe. My shoulders feel so heavy, as if the weight of the world is upon my shoulders. My fists ball up, and I shake in agony as the intense pain of his loss relentlessly bursts through my body.

The pain is something that I think will remain forever. But my hope is that it will lessen over time through prayer, surrender, and God's healing hand. Over ten years have passed, and yet the pain remains the same. Some say time heals all wounds, but I disagree. Over time we learn to cope with the pain. We carry on living as best as we can. But the truth is that life will *never* be the same because there is a void. When Bobby died, a part of me died with him. Bobby had my heart, and when his soul left this earth, he took a piece of my heart with him. That piece of my heart is eternally his and the memories I have of him are eternally mine. Some memories are beautiful, while others are very painful. So with that being said, I'll walk you through our story from start to finish. My hope is that people can see and understand my perspective. My love for him was so immense because I believed that he was my soul mate. When others pushed me to "move on" or "get over it," I simply wasn't able to. I will say that I have tried my best to live on, and over time, I have adjusted to life without him.

The Beginning

I was born in California and grew up moving back and forth between Los Angeles, California, and Las Vegas, Nevada. I come from literally nothing. I had a rough and traumatic childhood but will save that history for another book. After my parents split, I lived with my mom until fifth grade. From then on, I lived back and forth between her and other family members, at least until my junior year of high school. At seventeen, I lived with my first boyfriend. After our relationship ended, I had a short stint where I was homeless, but by the grace of God, I wasn't out on the streets. I met my sponsor, Molly, through a recovery group called Celebrate Recovery hosted by Central Christian Church in Henderson, Nevada. Molly helped me and provided me with a roof over my head. She somehow paid for me to live in an extended stay hotel called Sienna Suites and essentially kept me off the streets. I lived there until I turned eighteen and could sign for an apartment of my own. I became close with Molly and a handful of other older women who became like mentors. I also became close with the lead pastor of Celebrate Recovery, Pastor Bob Wood, along with his wife, Karrie, and his sister Debbie. I was the youngest one to attend Celebrate Recovery but was a part of two groups. One group was led by Karrie Wood who guided me and a small group of other women through the twelve-step process of recovery. The second and primary group for me was led by Debbie Wood and was a group for survivors of physical, sexual, and emotional abuse, all of which I experienced throughout my childhood. Molly sponsored me, and I considered her to be an angel that God strategically placed in my life. Pastor Bob, Karrie, Debbie, Molly, and a handful of other courageous women became my church family. I learned so much from them, and they positively impacted my youth. They inspired me and kept me off the streets, which I will forever be grateful for.

When I turned eighteen, Molly helped me get into an apartment down the street from my school. Through Molly's community resources, she got me a small grant to use at Big Lots. She took me shopping for basic essentials such as cooking utensils, pots, pans, bedding, and a small futon bed. She was also able to help me get some used furniture from a program with her job. I didn't have much, but I was thankful that God provided me with a place of my own—a place I wouldn't be kicked out of, a place where I felt safe. However, I still had to do my part of paying the rent and bills. I struggled. I attended high school and worked two, sometimes three, part-time jobs to pay my rent and bills. I had no car, so I rode the city bus to and from work. Sometimes I was able to get a ride from my best friend, Rodrigo, or other friends. I often had to choose between hot water and electricity because my checks weren't very much. I always chose electricity because my stove was electric, and I didn't want what little food I had in the fridge to go to waste. Not going to lie, the cold showers really sucked, especially at night. Honestly though, I was happy with the fact that I had a roof over my head and a warm bed to sleep in. Being that I was labeled homeless, my school offered free breakfast and lunch, but I never got to school in time for breakfast, and my last class was right before lunch, so I chose to go to work instead.

My friend Edgar used to comment that my fridge was always empty, but I was too prideful to let anyone know that I was struggling. I would simply say that I just needed to go shopping. I told him I worked a lot and never had the time. Edgar would walk me to school every morning because he lived right down the street. At times, I had apples or oranges because they were cheap. Edgar would always grab a piece of fruit if I had it, but I never complained because I never wanted to admit that I was struggling. I was great at hiding things, even if it was in plain sight. My best friend, Rodrigo, would often buy me dinner. Thankfully, I usually went to sleep with a full belly. Weekends were the best because after work, I would hang out with Edgar, Rodrigo, and our other friends, Gabby and Monique. I stayed out of trouble hanging out with them. We had fun, and they always kept me fed. Anytime Rodrigo bought pizza, he'd leave what was left over, and I'd always make that last. I didn't have a microwave, but pizza tastes good cold. My small circle became like family until we grew up and naturally went our separate ways.

Unfortunately, my struggles reflected in my grades. I also had to give up playing sports so that I can work as many hours as possible. The drop in my GPA and loss of sports resulted in no scholarships for college. It seemed like all the doors were closing on me. All I knew was that I was determined to make something of myself somehow, some way. I was adamant about not turning out like my parents who both turned to the gang life early on. My parents made some very poor life choices, which led to my traumatic childhood. I didn't have role models as parents. Instead, they taught me so much about who I didn't want to be. Because of my parents, I kept myself on a straight path. I was determined to be successful in life. Therefore I am grateful for my parents and the environment that I was raised in. They motivated me to stay away from drugs, to be independent, and to make better life choices. Because of the trauma I experienced as a result of their poor choices, I have made it a point to break our generational curses and to pave the path of success for my future bloodline. God made me different. I stood out from a young age. At first I hated it because I never felt like I fit in, especially with my own family. Looking back, I understand why. I experienced pain and turned it into a passion for change, a passion for a better way of life. I'm well on my way toward accomplishing that. Drugs, alcohol, and abuse all ran through my family until it ran into me. God is helping me break the cycle, and I am extremely determined to do just that. It stops with me but not without struggle.

My older brother had joined the army a year or two prior and was doing really good. At the time, I looked up to my brother. I had literally followed in his footsteps since we were kids. If he played sports, so did I. When he joined wrestling, so did I, despite being the only girl on the team. He hated it and thought I was annoying.

When we were younger, I wanted to be just like him, and throughout the years, I yearned for his approval despite our dysfunctional relationship. To be honest, I never thought I'd join the military. I always dreamt of going to college and becoming a nurse, but life has never gone as planned.

Naturally, I followed in my brother's footsteps, so in March of 2008, I walked into the recruiting station to start the enlistment process. My brother wanted me to go to college, then get in as an officer. I didn't have the funds for that, so I did what I had to do to make something of myself. I warned my recruiter Staff Sergeant Flores not to lie or bullshit me because my brother was already in. Staff Sergeant Flores laughed but was cool about it and remained honest with me from the start. I told him I wanted to be a medic. Unfortunately, I couldn't get in as a medic because my Armed Services Vocational Aptitude Battery (ASVAB) scores weren't high enough. Instead, Staff Sergeant Flores recommended I join as a 42A. I had no idea what that was. He explained that it was a desk job, and he thought I'd be great at it. He was also able to get me a small bonus. Since I wasn't able to be a medic like I wanted, I said screw it and signed up for it. Honestly though, I am thankful that he chose a Military Occupational Specialty that I was able to learn a lot from, that I enjoyed most of my career, and that transitioned well into the civilian sector.

I graduated from Basic High School in June of 2008. Being that I was still labeled as homeless, my school paid for my cap and gown along with my yearbook and my grad night trip to Disneyland. Most of my friends didn't attend grad night, so I hopped on the bus alone. Thankfully I was able to find some acquaintances to enjoy grad night with. A week later, I was on my way to Basic Combat Training (BCT), which many know as boot camp. I arrived at Fort Jackson, South Carolina, late at night. I immediately questioned my life decisions when the drill sergeants (DS) jumped on the bus and started screaming at us to "get the fuck off the bus!" We were rushed out and had to dump our bags so they could get rid of any contraband before we were assigned a bunk for the night. I don't think we went to bed until around 11:00 p.m. or so. The next day, around 4:00 a.m., I awoke to female Drill Sergeants screaming to get our "lazy asses" out of bed. I learned to move quickly because we were rushed to do everything. We were in reception for a few days where we went through many different stations and were issued our uniforms and boots. The vision station issued, if needed (which unfortunately I did), a pair of big ugly square-shaped brown plastic-framed glasses to wear for the duration of boot camp. Thankfully, we were also issued inserts for our eye gear, which I kept on most of the time to avoid wearing those huge ugly glasses. We had our first PT test during reception, but it was a condensed version: one minute of sit-ups, one minute of push-ups, and a one-mile run. I got scared because I was called out by Drill Sergeant Chadwick who was my grader. He pointed me out and said, "She can PT!" He called out a few other people too. I didn't understand what he meant, and it scared me because I didn't want to bring attention to myself.

Afterward, our names were called out, and we were assigned to one of three platoons. My platoon was led by three infantry Drill Sergeants: Drill Sergeant Lightner, Drill Sergeant Chadwick, and Drill Sergeant Worthington. All three had very different personalities, and they all had different "triggers" that would result in us getting smoked the crap out of. Getting smoked was basically a form of punishment by means of excessive exercise in various forms (mostly push-ups) that resulted in muscle failure. Because I "stood out," I was placed in leadership position as a squad leader, and that is how I met my friend Logan. We were assigned to the same platoon and were both assigned as squad leaders.

Drill Sergeant Worthington taught quite often and had a short temper. His favorite word seemed to be *simultaneously* because he said it all the time. When he smoked us, he made us do "little man in the woods," which was an exhausting form of exercise. We were to hold our rifle over our head in a low squatting position. With our legs only, we were to mimic jumping jacks but maintain the low squatting position. Drill Sergeant Lightner came off as the worst of the three and, in my opinion, was the one I was most scared of. He was always serious and always talked crap to us while the other two at least joked here and there. However, at the end of the cycle, we got to see another side of Drill Sergeant Lightner. He was a normal human being for once, and he actually gave half a smile. Drill Sergeant Lightner had gotten married during our cycle to another Drill Sergeant, and his wife was pregnant. I remember one night she and another female Drill Sergeant from a different platoon woke up all the females around midnight and smoked us all for about an hour. Rumor had it she was craving something, and Drill Sergeant Lightner had duty that night so he couldn't get it for her, so she smoked us for it. Never knew what the real reason was as to why we got smoked.

All I knew was female Drill Sergeants smoked us a lot worse than the males hands down, at least until the one time we really pissed off Drill Sergeant Chadwick. Drill Sergeant Chadwick was the laid-back one of the three and had the best army stories, but man, if you pissed him off, he surely had another side. I remember he was really mad at the platoon for whatever reason, so he smoked us. DS Chadwick made us do push-ups, lunges, sprints, flutter kicks, burpees, and he made us "roll left and roll right" all over the ground. It was terrible. I legit felt like I was going to puke, and I was terribly sore.

Drill Sergeant Bessy was another Drill Sergeant in our company but was in charge of a different platoon. He scared the crap out of me too but only because he would mess with us. Prime example, one day at the Dining Facility (DFAC), Drill Sergeant Bessey grabbed a piece of cake and asked a few of us if we wanted it. He kept saying, "Just take it!" Yeah, hell no! At the time, we could not have sweets or even dressing on our salads. He would test us to see if anyone would take the bait and then laugh because we were all too scared. The final week of training, I wrote a speech about our experience was able to read it at mass during Catholic service. I was unsure of the other Christian denominational church services offered to us, so I attended Catholic Mass with Logan and a few others. I wrote about our Drill Sergeants and made a joke about getting smoked all the time. Someone had told Drill Sergeant Chadwick about it, and he came up to me and asked me about it. No lie, I got really scared. I thought I was going to get yelled at or smoked. Drill Sergeant Chadwick made me give him the paper I wrote, and after he read it, he chuckled and told me to get out of his face. Our Drill Sergeants were awesome, assholes, but awesome nonetheless! Drill Sergeant Chadwick and Drill Sergeant Lightner became two Non-Commissioned Officers (NCO) that I truly looked up to after reconnecting later on down the road.

Right after basic training, Logan and I attended Advanced Individual Training (AIT) together. AIT was the training that focused specifically on the particular job that we would be doing in the army. We were both 42As, Human Resources Specialists. In AIT, we bunked right next to each other, and by the end of training, we had become close friends. At the end of training, we received our orders for our first duty station. I wanted to go to Fort Hood because my older brother was stationed there, but God had other plans for me. Logan and I both got orders for Fort Carson, Colorado, and I was excited that she would be there with me. God knew what he was doing when he placed her in my life, and to be honest, I needed her throughout everything that had happened. I am so thankful she was by my side every step of the way. She became my best friend and a sister for life.

Meeting Bobby Justin Pagan

I was eighteen and fresh out of Basic Training and AIT. I reported to Fort Carson, Colorado, November of 2008. My friend Logan was already there and had signed in a few days before me. We were in reception, which was kind of like a transition process to integrate us on to the base. We stayed in their temporary barracks, which is like a dorm room but for soldiers and not as nice. A week or two later, we would be sent to our assigned units.

Logan had met this guy named Bailey, and one evening, she and I went to eat dinner at the DFAC, a military cafeteria. As we were leaving, Logan stopped by a booth full of guys to say hi to her friend Bailey. Bobby was sitting at the table with them in the left inside corner of the booth. Logan introduced me, and Bailey tried to say my last name but failed. He had this thick country accent, but most people butchered my last name anyway, so I laughed. Bobby spoke up and loudly said, "Soriano!" He even rolled the *R* and everything! He caught my eye right then and there. My smile is just as big now thinking back on it, as it was on the day that we met. I pointed to him and said, "Yeah, you said it right," but I couldn't hide the huge smile on my face. Bobby smiled back. Bailey said something smart, but I can't remember what it was because Bobby had stolen my attention. Whatever he said, the whole table laughed. I read the name tape on Bobby's uniform, and it said *Pagan*. After that, Logan said bye, I told them it was nice to meet them, and we left. We didn't have a car at the time, so we walked a couple blocks back to the reception barracks.

As we were walking, Logan got a text and said, "Hey, Raino." That was her nickname for me. "Pagan wants your number."

I was like, "Who?"

She said, "The guy who said your last name, Bailey's friend. He's asking for your number."

At first, I said, "Hell no!" but Logan always used to push me out of my comfort zone to try to get me out of my shell. By the time we got back to the barracks, I said, "Okay, you can give him my number," and she did.

Pagan texted me shortly after asking me how I was doing that evening. Naturally, I responded with "Who's this?" And he said, "It's Pagan. I met you earlier with your homegirl, Logan." We spent the rest of the night texting each other, and he asked me if I wanted to meet up with him that weekend at a club. There was a club in downtown Colorado Springs called Pure 13 that was popular back then and allowed people ages eighteen and up to get in (I don't believe it exists anymore). I agreed and told Logan so that we could go together.

The First Date

During reception, we weren't supposed to go out past 10:00 p.m. Bobby and his friends were already with their respective units, so curfew didn't apply to them anymore. So what did we do? Logan, our new friend Javonna, and I literally snuck out of the reception barracks to go to Pure 13! Those two girls were down to do just about anything, and we are all still good friends to this day. There was another girl named Morgan who was going to go with us, but when the cab pulled up, she got scared and went back into the barracks. So the three of us jumped in the cab and off we went.

The girls and I were all under twenty-one at the time. We were allowed to go into the club, but the bouncers would use a black Sharpie and write a huge, embarrassing X on both our hands before we could enter. Best believe we went straight to the bathroom and tried to scrub it all off! After trying our best to scrub off the Xs from our hands, which never really worked, we went to the dance floor and had a good time. I didn't see Bobby all night until midnight when the club closed for underaged people. The people twenty-one and older could go to the bar side of the club that remained open until 2:00 a.m., but everyone with the X on their hands had to leave. As we were walking out, Bobby walked up with some girl and shouts, "Hey, Logan!" That dang girl had her left arm around Bobby's shoulder, and he had his right arm around her lower back. I stood there next to Logan while she said hi, and this dude didn't say a dang thing to me! He looked straight at me and then turned and walked into the twenty-one and older side with ol' girl. Bobby was twenty-one. I was like "No, he didn't!" I laugh now thinking back on it, but I wasn't laughing that night. I was pissed.

We left and caught a cab back to post (the army base). I had a good time dancing, so the night wasn't wasted, but I told Logan he can lose my number. We got back to the barracks and snuck back in. As soon as I lay down on my bed, I got a text from Bobby asking me why I didn't show up. Needless to say, he got cussed out over text. So he called me and said he didn't see me at all. I told him that I was standing right next to Logan when he said hi and then walked off with that tall freaking girl (she was literally about his height). He laughed! He had a cute laugh, but I wasn't having it. He swore he didn't see me and thought I stood him up. I was like, "Yeah right!" I told him I didn't have time for his BS and to lose my number. Then I hung up on him. He bugged me the rest of week. He blew up my phone asking me to give him another chance, but I kept standing my ground and saying no every single time. Logan said I was hardheaded and kept pushing me to give him another chance as well. You were supposed to be on my side, Lolo!

The following Saturday night, he called and asked if I could meet him at the club again. I said, "Hell no! I'm not repeating what happened the last time." I told him he blew it, but he was persistent and asked, "Okay, how about the movies then?" I said, "I'm not going unless Logan goes." So to my surprise, Bobby set up a double date with his friend Nelson for the next day. We went to the movies to see *Transporter 3*. I wore a long sleeve gray turtleneck dress that accentuated my curves. I had my hair down and curled and wore light makeup like always. He borrowed his friend Macias' car and picked us up to go to the movies. It was a white two-door car, so they had to get out to let us in and out of the back seat. When Bobby seen me, he said, "Damn, you do look different out of uniform!" I looked up at him, squinted, and said, "Not that different!" He just laughed.

Personally, I felt like the army uniform made me look fat, but that dress definitely accentuated my little curves. Bobby had on a pair of jeans, a Tap Out shirt, and a matching hat that he wore backward but with the brim facing a little to the left side. He looked good too, let me tell you! When we got to the theater, I was nervous and started to feel my face warm up. He paid for the tickets and for our snacks while Nelson paid for Logan and himself. I was holding the popcorn. There was a preview for a scary movie and I jumped, spilling the popcorn everywhere! Bobby busted up laughing. I slapped his shoulder and told him to shut up and stop laughing, but he didn't. He learned right then and there that I should never hold the popcorn. We watched the movie, and then they took us back to the base because it was dark by the time we got out of the theater. We spent the rest of the night talking on the phone. He kept giving me crap and making fun of me for jumping during the preview, but man, I loved hearing his laugh. It made me melt inside, and he put a huge smile on my face. Logan said she liked him and that she had a good time as well. Just like that, Bobby was back in my good graces and won me back over again.

The next morning, we got sent to our units and were placed in our unit barracks. Bobby, Logan, Bailey, and Javonna all ended up in the same brigade, 4th Infantry Brigade Combat Team. They were in different companies and battalions within the brigade, of course, but they were all in the same overall unit. I was placed in 3rd Brigade, in a Special Troops Battalion. Morgan (the girl who was too scared to sneak out) ended up being my roommate. She also worked in the same office as me, which was cool. At least I knew someone. Bobby kept texting me throughout the day and calling me in the evenings that week. We talked about everything from where we were from, to our reasons for joining the army, how we felt about our units so far, and of course, what sports teams we liked. He was a Dallas Cowboys fan, and I grew up as a Raiders fan. Of course, he made fun of me for it! (Don't hate Raider Nation, y'all!)

That weekend, he asked if he could walk over to my barracks, which were a few blocks away from his. Poor guy walked in the snow that Saturday evening to come see me, but we sat and talked for hours. I really, really liked him. I liked the confidence he had. Bobby had mentioned that he wasn't looking for anything serious, and honestly, I wasn't either. I had just gotten there after all. Yet before he left that night, he asked if we could go on a second date on Sunday afternoon to a pizza place on the base that played football games on the big screen. I think it was called Godfather's Pizza but don't quote me. It was a big building off the corner of Specker and Prussman next to the small car dealership. It close enough for us to walk to from the barracks. I said yes, of course, and then Bobby walked all the way back to his room in the snow at like ten or eleven at night. Poor guy, neither one of us had a car at the time, and I know it was cold that night, but he wanted to see me, so he did.

That Sunday, around eleven in the morning, Bobby walked over to my room, and we walked to the pizza place up the street. He bought me lunch, and we talked/argued over football. He let me know that Demarcus Ware and Miles Austin were his favorite players and that my team "just sucked ass." Bobby was very competitive and very good with stats. I quickly learned that no matter what I said, he always had a dang comeback. Bobby would just laugh when I'd get flustered or frustrated. We also talked about the states we were from and argued over which one was better, California or Texas. I for sure argued every point as to why I thought California was better. Bobby simply said, "The state ain't great if it don't got an X in it." Then he made fun of the California state flag. He said that we had Yogi Bear on our state flag and that we had nothing on Texas! Then he rubbed it in by informing me that the Texas state flag is the *only* flag that can fly as high as the American flag. I just kept laughing at the Yogi Bear comment. Bobby sure knew how to make me laugh!

That day, we talked about sports, different types of music we liked, different music artists that we liked, and so much more. I told him Tupac was my favorite rapper, Bone Thugs-N-Harmony was my favorite group, and that I absolutely loved Motown oldies because that was the music I was raised listening to. Bobby listened to everything but was a big R&B fanatic. I learned that he loved Jagged Edge, and he claimed to be their fifth member, but they just didn't know it yet! We were there for hours, just talking, arguing, and laughing with each other. We were both all smiles. I smiled so much my cheeks hurt.

Afterward, Bobby walked me back to my barracks. Then he leaned in, and we had our first kiss. His lips were so soft, big, and juicy, especially his bottom lip! Man, he was a great kisser. Hell, I got butterflies just thinking about it. Honestly though, to say I had butterflies that day is an understatement! After that, we spent every day together after work just talking and hanging out. I didn't have a TV yet, so we would just order food, watch movies on my laptop, and hang out. Being that he was a gentleman, he would always come to me so that I never had to walk in the snow. He never complained either, but I know it was cold as hell at night. Colorado winters are no joke.

Making It Official

I became accustomed to the way things worked in my unit and quickly caught on to the job. My first Non-Commissioned Officer (NCO) was Sergeant Goodwin, who had just come back from Iraq after getting pregnant on deployment, but she chose not to keep the baby. She was cool and was a friendly NCO. I really liked her at first until I realized she took advantage of me. I was a private and was dumb and naive when it came to not knowing what we could and couldn't say no to. At that time in the army, we were not to ask questions we were just to do as we were told, and unfortunately, my NCO took advantage of that. She had me cosign for a Chevy Trailblazer that she bought, and she had me add a phone line to my T-Mobile account for her. She recognized my abilities through my work ethic and voiced how far I could go in the military, but for a while, I was unsure if she meant it or if it was because I essentially "helped" her. For about two weeks, she placed me in charge of the shop while she was out. I was a private (E-2) in charge of two specialists and two Private First Class Soldiers, at least until the specialists finally stepped it up. For a while I thought my NCO and I were friends because we hung out outside of work from time to time. That was my mistake, but she was also wrong for what she did. It wasn't until the rest of our shop returned from Iraq that I realized what she asked me to do was unlawful. Someone told Staff Sergeant Ramos what I did for Sergeant Goodwin, and I was questioned about it. At first, I was scared, not going to lie, because Staff Sergeant Ramos intimidated me. I didn't want to get in trouble, so I said no at first but then I folded and admitted that it was true. I called Sergeant Goodwin and warned her.

She freaked out and said, "No, no, my phone isn't under your name, and the truck is mine." I said, "It's me you are talking to, Umm... Hello, your phone is a line under my account." In a matter of minutes, she had her own phone line, but she couldn't change the fact that I cosigned on the Trailblazer. Looking back, I can't believe I allowed that to happen, but again, I was a private and didn't know any better. It's because of her that I was always wary of female NCOs, especially the "cool" ones. It is because of her and the other female NCOs that I came across that I preferred to be a no-nonsense NCO, and I always cared about the wellbeing of my soldiers. We'll get back to that later in the story though.

Sometime in December of 2008, my NCO invited me and our squad over to her house for dinner and drinks. Yes, a couple of us were underage, and yes, it was technically against the rules, but it turned out to be more common than I thought. Combat units are kind of different in a sense. The basic rules still applied to us, but people had the mindset that if you can fight for your country, then you can have a drink. As long as we were all responsible and could understand that in the office, we were to remain professional and not discuss weekend activities that went on, then we were good. So I went, hung out with the girls, and had a few drinks. Bobby checked up on me and asked if I was having a good time. I told him I was good and asked how long he was going to stay up (it was kind of late). He said if I wanted to, I could go over, and he'd wait up for me. I had never been to his room before, he had only been to mine, and so I agreed. When the party was over, the girls drove me to his barracks. Being that it was an all-male barracks, my roommate Morgan decided to walk with me up to his room where he was waiting by the door. She did the typical girl thing, threatened him, and told him to take care of me. He promised he would, and he did. I wasn't drunk, I had a light buzz but was still very aware of what I was doing. Bobby gave me some water and made sure I was okay anyway. We laid there in his bed talking and laughing, and well, eventually we started kissing and one thing led to another. Bobby slowly and gently took care of me in another way. I'll spare the details because I'm pretty sure my parents might read this, or family members, possibly his family too, and well, that's just awkward. Needless to say, that night was amazing, and the next morning, he was such a gentleman. He walked me home and he asked if I was okay with what had happened or if I had any regrets. He said if I did, we didn't have to do it again, that he could wait. Now honestly that happened kind of early in the relationship. I had made my ex before him wait a whole year. Bobby and I had only known each other a month, yet I did not regret it, not at all.

That same December, my grandma passed away, and I went home for her funeral. Before I left, I had discussed my family dynamic with Bobby. We were a very dysfunctional family to say the least. Bobby spent the night with me in my room that night, and I was emotional. I had flipped over and turned away from him so that I could cry silently like I normally would in my past. I *hate* crying, especially in front of other people. I don't know if he had seen the tears well up in my eyes or heard the change in my breathing, but Bobby wouldn't allow it. He pulled my shoulder back until I was flipped all the way over facing him again. I kept my face down, in the crevasse of his neck. Bobby told me to look at him, but I said no, so he gently grabbed my chin and lifted my face so that our eyes met. He told me it was okay to cry and assured me that he was there for me. He told me that he would be my shoulder to cry on whenever I needed him to be. I told Bobby that my mom instilled in me that it was weak to cry and that because of it, I hated crying in front of people. I hated showing weakness. Bobby told me that I should never be ashamed to cry, especially in front of him. He held me close and told me to let it out, so I did. I held tightly on to him, and I cried into his chest until I felt better. We weren't even official, but I swear I loved him right then and there. No one ever cared enough to do that for me. Bobby made sure that I knew it was perfectly fine to express my emotions. He wanted to be the one who could console me, help me through it, and then make me laugh so I could feel better. No one had ever broken it down like that nor had anyone ever done that for me before. No one ever cared enough, but Bobby did.

From then on out, he wanted me to express my emotions and trust that he would be there to support me. When I flew back to Las Vegas, Bobby checked up on me throughout the whole time I was there. After I had explained the dynamic of my family to him, he was worried about me. My family is very dysfunctional, and I never really felt like I fit in. However, when I went home to visit that time, it was actually a good visit. It was the first time my family had seen me in my Class A uniform, and some of my family members told me they didn't even know I joined the military. My older brother and I finally seen each other in uniform, and of course, my mom made us take pictures together. My dad was in jail at the time, but my mom attended the funeral with us and paid her respects to my grandma. It snowed in Las Vegas that year, which was rare but awesome. I spent a few days with my family, and it went well for the most part. I flew back to Colorado on December 19th, and on my way back, Bobby asked me about the status of our relationship. I told him I knew we were technically just friends and that I knew he wasn't looking for anything serious.

However, I admitted that I really enjoyed his company and that I really liked him. He asked, "Do you have any other friends like me?" I knew what he was implying, and I said, "No Pagan, you're the only guy I'm talking to." He said, "Good," and then he asked me right then and there to be his girlfriend. My heart filled with joy, and I immediately said yes! So that was it, December 19, 2008, we officially became a couple.

Head over Heels

Christmas was coming up, and we both ended up staying in Colorado for the holidays. Typically, soldiers have the chance to take leave and go home. I made plans to go to my coworker Robinson's house for Christmas to exchange gifts for our shop's Secret Santa. I asked if Bobby could tag along, and of course she said yes. I should have planned better and got him a gift for Christmas, but he told me last minute that he wasn't going home, and I had already gone shopping for the Secret Santa gift. I didn't have a car, so I frantically tried to come up with a gift. I just wanted him to have something to open. Christmas morning came, and I asked Rob for a ride to the store on post, but literally everything was closed, even the shoppette. I remembered I had some random football jersey for who knows what team that a friend had gifted, so it still had tags on it. It wasn't a Raiders jersey nor was it a Cowboys jersey, but I wrapped it up so he would have something to open. Terrible, I know! When he opened it, he laughed and looked at me, confused because it wasn't his team. I said, "I know it's not your team, babe. I just wanted you to have something to open so that you didn't feel left out." The smile on his face was priceless; he really appreciated the gesture. I never did see that jersey again!

My NCO was there and invited all of us to go to her house for New Year's Eve, so we made plans to go and ring in the New Year together. On New Year's Eve, I wore a nice black dress that hugged my body, and he wore a white button-down shirt with a black T-shirt under. He was fine too! They picked us up, and we had a great time at her house. That night, we took our first picture together ringing

29

in the New Year (2009), and he sent the picture to his mom. It was a great time, and things only got better from then on out. I felt so lucky. In my eyes, Bobby was handsome, he had a great personality, he was a gentleman, he always made me laugh, he was great in bed, and we had great conversations! He was a great catch, and I knew it. Bobby kept telling me he was the lucky one, and that night he told me he loved me. Man, little did he know I had already fallen head over heels for him!

A couple weeks after New Year's and right before my nineteenth birthday, his unit had to pack up and go to training for a month down in Fort Polk, Louisiana. I was sad that he was going to miss my birthday, but Bobby made me feel better about it and said he would make up for it when he got back. He was so cute. He gave me the key to his barracks room and said I could go there any time that I missed him. His pillow and blankets smelled like him so he said that might help me feel better. Bobby wore a lot of Axe. He had multiple scents, but his favorite to wear was the chocolate-scented Axe, and I actually liked it too. Unfortunately, they weren't coming back until the week after Valentine's Day, so we would be missing our first Valentine's Day together as well.

During that month, my older brother called and said that I could use his car for a year while he was deployed in Iraq. I just had to take over payments and find a way to pick up the car from my mom in Las Vegas, where he had left it. One of my coworkers, either Dozier or Rob, had helped rent a car for me since I was too young to get it myself. My roommate Morgan drove down with me to Las Vegas so that I could drive the car back while she drove the rental back. By then, Morgan and I had become a little closer after confiding in each other and sharing some slight similarities in childhood traumas. She was the first person who got to meet my parents and didn't mind accompanying me on the twelve-hour drive to Las Vegas. I got my first traffic ticket on the way home for speeding. I was nervous and pulled over on the wrong side of the road. The cop yelled at me but essentially let us go. When we got to Vegas, Morgan got to meet my parents. My dad was living in a halfway home, and I was honestly embarrassed. She was cool about it though, and I appreciated that. My brother had a black 2007 Chevy Impala, and I loved it. I couldn't wait to surprise Bobby when he got back so that we could start venturing out more and so he wouldn't have to walk in the snow anymore to come see me. Not that he ever complained, he really didn't, but I could now pick him up and drop him off once he got back.

For Valentine's Day, I went with my friend Kortney who was a coworker of mine, and we got a bunch of Valentines decorations. Shortly after Kortney arrived at the unit, we just clicked. I honestly don't think she liked me at first, but then she said something along the lines of "real recognize real," and over time, we became close friends. Kortney was a very straightforward person who didn't sugar-coat anything and had no filter. I loved her! I was the same way.

I wanted to decorate Bobby's room for Valentine's Day to sur-prise him when he got back, so Kortney helped me out. She also made me go to a sex shop for the first time ever; it was located on B Street right outside the gate. Not going to lie, I was low-key scared, but we laughed at the different items in the store, and she gave me the 411 on a few things. I ended up getting some massage oil and a couple of outfits that she made me try on and said I had to get. I was still self-conscious about my body. Kortney was this fabulously confident person who just wasn't having it. She boosted my self-es-teem and told me that I looked great in the outfits. I told her I wasn't comfortable in those skimpy outfits and that I felt stupid. She said, "Girl, you just gotta go with it and be open to shit." Kortney said Bobby was going to love seeing me in the outfits and then gave me an ultimatum. She said, "Either you buy them, or I will!" She was so serious, so I bought them. I was really shy when it came to stuff like that, but Kortney helped me come out of my shell.

The Promise Ring

The four weeks Bobby was away for training felt like forever. It didn't help that everyone in my barracks kept getting in trouble because people couldn't keep the barracks clean. One Friday night, we had a GI party, which was basically when we had to sweep, mop, buff, and clean the entire barracks building from top to bottom and left to right. We started on the bottom floor and worked our way up to the third floor. I was mad as hell. We had a bunch of dirty people living in our barracks, and it certainly showed. My roommate was hooking up with the Staff Sergeant in charge of the barracks, and he happened to be hosting the GI party. Basically, she wasn't doing anything because they disappeared into an empty room for majority of the time. We slowly started drifting apart once they started messing around because he was married with kids, and I essentially didn't support their relationship.

Toward the end of the GI party, Kortney and I got stuck sweeping and mopping our hall on the third floor. Some guy pissed me off because he was up there but wasn't helping, yet he felt the need to say something slick. I cussed him out, then angrily mopped the floor. Guys in the military can be jerks, and they can say some off-the-wall unnecessary stuff. I always had to prove myself for the simple fact that I was female serving in the military. I definitely had a temper back then too and was kind of a loose cannon if I was upset, especially around other lower enlisted personnel. I didn't take crap from anyone. NCOs were another story though. I didn't dare give attitude to any NCOs, at least not in the beginning and most certainly not in that unit.

Anyway, Kortney kept trying to calm me down, but I was mad as hell. Then she said, "Diana, look up." She was literally the only person who ever called me by my first name. I stubbornly and angrily said no. Kortney said "Diana, turn around," and again, I said no and kept mopping. But I looked up and turned my head anyway.

Bobby was standing at the end of the hallway by the stairwell in front of my room. He had a huge smile on his face. In his right hand, he was holding a single red rose with a small piece of baby's breath nestled in a thin glass vase. I threw the mop down and ran into his arms. I was so happy to see him that I couldn't even say anything. I just cried. It was probably a mixture of frustration from the night and having missed him, but I was finally back in his arms. He hugged me so tight and then kissed me as he wiped the tears off my cheeks. I could hear Kortney in the background laughing, and then she said, "Aww, y'all cute."

Bobby laughed and then told me he would wait in my room while I finished up. Man, I've never been so happy to mop up some floors let me tell you! I was motivated to finish so that I could get back to my man! We finally finished up after what felt like forever and got the approval to be released for the evening. I couldn't get back to my room fast enough! Bobby was waiting for me on the bed. When I walked in, he got up, hugged me, and asked me to put a movie on for us to watch while he used the bathroom really quick. His hat was on my laptop. Normally I would've picked up the hat and placed it on the dresser, but for some reason, I slid his hat off and started looking up a movie for us to watch.

When he walked back in, he smacked his lips annoyed and said, "Babe, did you pick up the hat?" I was confused and said, "No, I slid it off. Why?" He smacked his lips again and said, "Babe, pick up my hat." Confused, I picked it up, and under it was a small blue box from Harris Jewelers. I immediately sucked in a big breath of air in surprise. Bobby stopped me though. He said, "Hold up. It's not what you think it is!" Then he grabbed the box, opened it, and said, "It's a promise ring. We are going to deploy soon. Do you think you can wait for me?" My heart skipped a beat, and I happily said, "Yes, of course I can!" Bobby asked, "Do you promise? You can't be messing with no other dudes while I'm gone." I said, "I promise papi, I'll wait for you!"

Then Bobby slid a beautiful white gold ring with three diamonds on my finger. It was a beautiful princess cut diamond ring. I knew right then and there he was the one for me. Bobby had told me that he had been planning his surprise and that Kortney had helped him out. Kortney later had jokingly told me that there was another ring, but I didn't believe her at the time because of the way that she said it. I thought she was joking, but we'll come back to that.

Being that I had his room key and it was already late, Bobby slept in my room that night. He passionately made love to me and whispered in my ear, "I just need you to wait for me." Again, I promised him that I would. My heart was set on him, and I knew in my heart that I didn't want anyone else. The next morning, I showed him the car, and we drove over to his room. I surprised him with his decorated room and one of the outfits I had bought just for him. Bobby absolutely loved it, and he helped me feel more comfortable about wearing the outfit in front of him as well. When I had initially come out of the bathroom in the outfit, I didn't want to show him. I was shy so I kept my arms crossed around my stomach and kept my head down. It was a very short two-piece army outfit. The top was made of a short green camouflage cloth and had black fishnet lace sewed in. The matching skirt was even shorter; the bottom of my butt was exposed. I was not comfortable showing off my body, even if he had seen me naked. Being naked under the covers or in the dark is completely different, I'm just saying. But anyway, Bobby sat on the bed and said, "Come here, ma" as he reached out for me with his left hand. When I walked up to him, he grabbed my arms and put them down to my sides. He looked into my eyes and said, "You are gorgeous, mami." Bobby always made me feel good about myself; he was great with reassurance. I ended up lighting the white tea light candles around his dresser, which illuminated the fake rose petals I had put around his room and bed and set the mood. Then I gave him a back massage with the massage oil I had bought. I'll skip the rest and continue on with the story. I'm sure you can guess what happened next.

At first, I was super shy around Bobby, especially when it came to exploring in the bedroom. I only had one serious relationship before him, so I wasn't very experienced, even though I had lived with my ex for a while. I loved that Bobby always made sure that I was comfortable, and because of it, I was open to trying new things with him. Bobby was a little older and a little more experienced than I was. He had also lived with an ex, Ticina, who eventually left and joined the Air Force. He told me that she got pregnant and told him it was his, but it turned out that the baby was someone else's child, and it broke his heart. Not only had she cheated, but the baby wasn't his. We were so open with each other about our pasts and some of the heartaches that we each experienced. I really appreciated that aspect of our relationship. I had told him about my ex whom I lost my virginity to in high school. Again, I didn't have a good family dynamic, so at seventeen, I lived with him until he cheated on me with my coworker. Then he kicked me out after our bad breakup. I had some serious trust issues that stemmed from my family and from my ex. But Bobby wanted to love me through it and earn my trust. Honestly, I wanted to do the same for him, so we did. It wasn't perfect, we had issues from time to time, but we always worked through it and constantly reassured each other. Bobby would tell me how much he admired my strength and would say I wasn't like anyone he had met before. He admired that I survived through everything that was made to break me yet still stood tall and always found a reason to smile. We both fell head over heels. So much for not wanting something serious!

The Impala

Bobby had great relationships with most people, especially his boys, and he was always offering to help them in any kind of way. Bobby convinced me to allow him to use the car sometimes because he wanted to be able to give his boys a ride to and from work. Something had happened with the car Macias had, and none of them had a car, so he wanted to be able to give his boys Macias, Bradley, Stringer, and sometimes Lopez a ride to work. I agreed to let him because Bobby only worked a block away from me, so the car rides weren't a big deal. Bobby would take the car to PT (physical training, basically the mandatory workout sessions) because my PT area was literally right outside my barracks and his was over by his company where he worked. Afterward, he would go to his room to shower and get ready for the day. Then Bobby and the boys would pile into the car and pick me up to take me to work. When he picked me up, he made it clear that whoever was in the front seat would have to get out and jump in the back when he pulled up so that I could sit in the front seat next to him. He always filled the tank, and sometimes, after lunch, Bobby would park in my work area parking lot. Bobby and the boys would walk through our building, and he'd knock on the door window of my office to get my attention. Bobby would smile and wave or would signal me to get up really quick so that he could sneak a kiss before he went back to work. It was cute, and the people in my shop would always bust my chops about it, especially because I'd always blush afterward.

 Everyone knew Pagan, and I loved that he would randomly do things to brighten up my day. Bobby would pick me up at the end of the day unless I told him that I was going to get a ride from Kortney; she lived two doors down from me. One morning, he was running late so when he pulled up, I just jumped in the back and told the person seated in the front to stay in the front so he could hurry up and get us all to work. I didn't want to get smoked for being late. As previously stated, getting smoked was a form of punishment by means of excessive exercise until muscle failure was achieved, and it completely sucked. Anyhow, I thought it was Macias sitting in the front, so I said, "Hey, Macias!" But he responded with "I'm not Macias!" Then I realized it was a white guy in the front, so I said, "My bad, Bradley!" They both laughed, and Bobby's friend Stringer turned around and said, "I'm not Bradley. I'm Stringer!" They never let me forget that, and it was a running joke for quite a while!

It was clear that we loved each other and took every opportunity to see each other or spend time together, even if it was only for a moment in passing. He was mine and everyone sure knew I was his! He used to love to sing the song "Bust It Baby" by Plies. His favorite part to sing was the chorus: "She got me speedin in the fast lane, pedal to the floor mayne, tryna get back to her love. Best believe she got that good thang, she my little hood thang, ask around they know us! They know that's mine, bust it, baby, everybody know that's mine!" Bobby also used to sing songs like "All My Life," "Kiss Me Thru the Phone," "Nobody," "I Wanna Know," and so much more, but his all-time favorite songs to sing to me were Jagged Edge songs. Some of his favorites to sing to me were "Promise," "I Gotta Be," "Good Luck Charm," "He Can't Love U," "Walked Outta Heaven," and of course, "Let's Get Married" (the original, not the remix). It didn't matter who was around, he would still sing to me. There was only one Spanish song that Bobby knew and would sing. It was called "Te Quiero" by Flex. Bobby told me that he used to work at a car dealership, and his coworker introduced him to the song. He would only sing the chorus, but I thought it was cute.

Bobby was mixed. He was Puerto Rican, Mexican, and Black, but he couldn't really speak Spanish. So when he sang the song to me, I thought it was adorable. After that, he would always ask me, "Si te quiero?" and I would always respond with "Si, te quiero, papi."

I honestly couldn't listen to Jagged Edge for years, but I've come to enjoy the songs again in his memory. I now have a playlist on Spotify just for him. It has all the songs that I remember him singing to or listening to during our car rides together. "Runnin My Momma Crazy" by Plies was a song that he loved and said reminded him of him and his mom and also "A Song for Mama" by Boyz II Men. He used to like singing and swaying to "Footprints" by T.O.K. as well. I can still picture him singing along, swaying from side to side, and lifting his hands over his head in a reggae-type dance at the stop lights.

I loved having Bobby drive me everywhere. Besides, my driving scared him! Academy was a long road, and I traumatized Bobby when Kortney and I used to race down Academy! She had a little red Chevy Cobalt with Betty Boop decorations all over the inside. We used to love to race each other. Bobby called us crazy and said he would be driving from then on. I just laughed, but I complied. Everyone said that was more of Bobby's car than mine. I used to be like "Yeah, right! I just let him drive it!" Once we had the Impala, we were out all the time. I really loved it! He would drive, hold my hand, and would sing to me. He wasn't bad either! Bobby mostly listened to '90s R&B when I was in the car especially Jagged Edge. He would sing and smile then would say, "I told you I'm the fifth member of Jagged Edge!" He also used to like singing to "Nice & Slow" by Usher, but when Usher spelled out his name, Bobby would replace the letters with his first and last name. So he would sing, "They call me BO-BBY PA-GA-N." I thought that was cute and would just giggle and smile every time he did it. Then he'd grab my hand and kiss it and continue holding it while he sang along to all the songs.

I'm not a good singer, but I would sing along with him for the girl parts when he played "Nobody" or "Twisted" by Keith Sweat, "Too Close" by Next, or "Nothing in this World" by KeKe Wyatt and Avant. Bobby loved Avant. His favorite Avant song was "Makin Good Love." He listened to hip-hop, rap, reggae, and even country music here and there, but he mostly played R&B around me. The boys would be around when he sang sometimes and Kortney as well. She used to egg him on, and he would tell her that she just didn't know that he was the fifth member of Jagged Edge. It is something

Kortney and I laugh about whenever we reminisce on the times we spent with Bobby. I don't remember if he ever sang in front of Logan, but I do remember he would for sure make fun of her, *all the time*.

Logan is a great runner, and she is originally from Liberia, so he would tease her and call her a gazelle. Bobby would tell her that she was so good at running because when she was a kid, she was out chasing the zebras. She would just laugh and call him an asshole. Bobby would just bust up laughing. Hell, we'd all be laughing at that point. Logan would always pick at me too, saying that my mom was pregnant with me in labor and waited to cross the border before she pushed me out so that I could be a citizen! People believed it too! Bobby used to say I was the little girl with the braids on the signs by the border, and I'd call him a fake Puerto Rican. We were terrible! We all used to always crack jokes about each other and talk crap to each other, but it was all out of love. Bobby liked my girls, and I liked his boys. It was always a good time no matter who we were around.

However, my favorite time was our alone time for the simple fact that I got to experience a side of Bobby that no one else did, his most loving side, and I adored him for it. Bobby was a tough guy, super competitive, and a manly man around the guys, but with me, he was a gentle giant. He had a heart of gold, and our intimate moments were very special. Bobby and I just connected on another level. It is so hard to try to depict in words the love we had experienced between each other. If people were around us, the love between us could be physically seen; there was no need for words. All I can say was that he was my soul mate, and he told me that I was his. We both knew that the love we had for each other was very special, and so did everyone around us. People go their whole lifetime in search of the type of love we shared. Yet there we were. We found true love at such a young age. It was truly beautiful, and I will forever cherish the love he gave me and everything that he taught me about love.

One time we were listening to Tupac and I rapped along to the whole song for "Brenda's Got a Baby" and "Dear Mama," he was impressed. I had told him, "I told you Tupac was my all-time favorite rapper!" Then the song "Picture Me Rollin" came on. He loved that song, especially at the end when Tupac said, "If you ever wanna see me again, just rewind this track, and picture me rollin!" Bobby said, "If I ever die, I want them to play Tupac at my funeral!" (Yeah, that didn't happen, but believe it or not, I mentioned it to his family.) He said he didn't want anyone to be sad or to cry over him at his funeral. (Yeah, that didn't happen either. A lot of people cried.) I had told him that if I ever died, I doubt that anyone would even show up to mine. My family and I weren't very close at all, and I always felt like most of them hated me anyway. That upset him, and he said he would be there if anything ever happened to me. I told him I wasn't sure what song I wanted played at my funeral, but if something ever happened to my brother, I knew what song I'd play for him. I told him I'd play "Good Riddance (Time of Your Life)" by Green Day because he used to play that song a lot, so it always reminded me of him. (Don't judge the song by its title, y'all. I know it sounds terrible, but listen to the song first before y'all come for me!)

One day, I had an argument with my mom. I told Bobby that if I ever died, I wanted the song "Leave Out All the Rest" by Linkin Park played specifically for my mother. I loved how we could talk about literally anything with each other and not think twice about it. He opened up to me, and I did the same with him. He made it so easy to confide in him about anything and everything. He made me feel safe and very loved.

The Ball

As previously stated, my unit had just come back from Iraq, so we had a military ball coming up. I asked Bobby if he wanted to go being that neither of us had been to a military ball before. He gladly accepted, but he wanted to wear a tux and not his uniform. Since he was going as my guest and wasn't in my unit, he was able to wear the tux. The unit happened to be trying to raise funds, so they allowed the female soldiers to wear dresses instead of uniforms, but for a fee. I gladly paid that fee, so when Bobby and I attended, neither of us were in uniform. Instead he wore a tux, and I wore a long gown. He was so handsome in his tux! The tux was comprised of black pants, a white long-sleeve shirt, a black vest, a black jacket, and a black bow-tie. My dress was a long strapless black ball gown with a white trim and silver crystals at the top. Kortney did my hair for me that night, and Bobby said I looked so beautiful. That night was so much fun, and we took pictures together.

One of my favorite pictures of him is when I caught him off guard. I held two fingers on his chest to stop him in his tracks and quickly snapped a picture of his gorgeous smile. We had a really great time, but the best part was being able to dance with him. The DJ was playing a mixture of music, and he was actually pretty good. I danced with Kortney for a couple of songs being that she dragged me to the floor as soon as he played "Stanky Legg"! That was our song! Bobby just sat and watched from the table laughing and shaking his head at us. When I came back to sit down, he was admiring the engraved wine glasses we drank from at our table, so I made sure to take them as a keepsake that night. When the DJ played "Too Close" by Next,

Bobby took my hand, led me to the dance floor, and we did our thing! It was followed by "Your Body's Callin" by R. Kelly. We were both all smiles and completely enjoyed the moment. The rhythm of those songs was a little more upbeat, so we weren't slow dancing. I was grinding a little on him and teasing him with my hips. He loved it! Although when I danced, it wasn't raunchy. It was playful and fun.

Then the DJ switched it up and played "Bump n' Grind." Bobby immediately started singing the lyrics and pulled me in close. That was our first and only slow dance. I swear it seemed as if everyone around us were nonexistent, and we shared that wonderful moment together on the dance floor. Bobby danced so sensually with me and leaned in and kissed me during the middle of our dance. He told me he loved me, and I told him I loved him more. It was beautiful, and I loved every moment of it. Bobby seriously took my breath away on the dance floor that night. After that song, we left the ball. We went back to my room and spent the rest of the night making love to each other. Whenever we were intimate in such a way, it was beautiful and endearing. Afterward he would caress me, and we would talk until we fell asleep in each other's arms. It was a perfect evening with the love of my life. A night that I will never forget and will forever cherish as a memory near and dear to me.

Living Together

One day, my coworker Dozier asked me if I could house sit for her and take care of her dog her while she and her husband went out of town. I agreed and asked her if it was okay if Bobby stayed with me at the apartment. She said it was fine if I had him there with me, so for about two to three weeks, we took over her apartment. Bobby usually stayed with me at my barracks, but living in the apartment was different because there was a kitchen. We didn't have to worry about getting caught in a random inspection, and it felt like a home. Technically guests were supposed to leave the barracks at 10:00 p.m., but Bobby never signed in nor did he ever leave. My room was adjacent to the side door exit, and people would always leave the door propped open with a rock or something so people would come and go as they pleased. Don't judge me. I wasn't the only one breaking all the rules.

Anyway, I cooked for him, and he cooked for me. There was one time when he attempted to make tacos, but even the dog wouldn't eat it! It was hilarious, but I appreciated the effort. I gave him so much crap for it though! Bobby tried to get me back by saying I burnt the meat on the previous meal, but he couldn't get me though. My comeback was the dog at least ate the leftovers when I cooked! One thing Bobby was great at was making really good tuna sandwiches. He had made tuna for me and shocked me when he put hardboiled eggs in it. I questioned him about it and gave him a weird facial expression. I had never seen it made that way nor had I eaten it like that before. He told me to trust him, and he was right, it was delicious! I've eaten my tuna that way ever since. It was nice because we had the opportunity to experience a glimpse of what it would be like to live together in a real home for future reference.

Bobby was very fond of the dog. He let me know he had a dog named Safira that his mom was taking care of while he was gone. He told me stories about her and said that he used to cook steaks just for his dog. He said his sisters used to come over and help him clean, and when he cooked, they would ask if the food was for them. He'd say no, that it was for Safira. He loved that dog and said he eventually wanted to go back to Texas for good and get her back from his mom. That's when we started talking about future plans to move back to Texas together. He was starting to picture his future with me in it, and I loved it. But he'd always crack jokes and said that if I got him mad, he was going to make me sleep on the couch while he cuddled in the bed with Safira instead! I said there is no way in hell I was going to let a dog take my spot on the bed I didn't care how mad he got at me, and he would just laugh about it. I miss his laugh so much.

One morning, we got into an argument in the apartment. I can't remember what the argument was about, but it was when I was hangry, so I'm pretty sure it was over something stupid. Bobby had brought back McDonalds for breakfast, and I remember being so mad I threw my Sausage McMuffin at his head. I was petty like that. He ducked, and I missed him, so the Sausage McMuffin hit the wall behind him and fell on the floor. The darn dog got to it before me, so there went my breakfast! Bobby kept laughing and teasing me, then made me clean up the mess from the crumbles and wrapper that remained. I can't remember exactly what he said, but he said something slick and made me laugh. Just like that, we were good! I told him I was hungry, but he said too bad, I shouldn't have thrown my breakfast at him. He said it was my own fault that the dog ate my food. He was such a turd! But he was right. Bobby let me have a bite of his food but stood his ground because I was in the wrong. I loved that Bobby was man enough to handle my attitude, which, let me tell you, can be pretty bad! He was kind and gentle with me but could easily put me in my place if the situation called for it, and I really loved that about him. He was not the type of man that you could walk all over, yet he always remained respectful with me, and I was extremely attracted to that.

Bobby was man enough to love me through the few rocky moments that we experienced and would always make me laugh. Anytime we got into an argument, he would say something stupid that would make me laugh, and the argument would be over just like that. I was such a brat, but he always handled me so well. Once he made me smile or laugh, I couldn't stay mad at him for anything. I mean seriously, I could never stay mad at him, like ever! I loved it. I asked him how he was so patient, and he would just say, "Babe, I got four sisters. They prepared me for this shit." Then he would tell me I better not ever mess up on him or he was gonna get his sisters on me and to trust him, he had four sisters waiting. I would just say, "I ain't scared of your sisters!" We were always jokingly going back and forth with each other. It was always a good time.

I loved spending time with him. I loved his sense of humor, his manliness, and his amazing character. What I admired most was how Bobby talked about his mom. He adored his mother and held her on a pedestal. She was his hero. His mom meant the world to him. Bobby looked up to her so much and loved her dearly. She was everything to him, and he wanted to repay her for everything that she had done for him but felt like it was an impossible task because she had done so much for him and his siblings. Bobby was a family man for sure!

When Dozier and her husband came back, they got upset because Bobby had watched porn on her husband's computer. Dozier's husband was a hacker-type dude and didn't like anyone touching his computer. I was so embarrassed. I didn't know that Bobby had gotten off early one day and watched porn on the dang computer. The worst part though was Dozier went back and told all the other girls in the office. I was mortified and so embarrassed. I called Bobby and was so angry with the situation. Especially because Dozier had a big mouth and told the whole shop, instead of keeping it just between us. I always hated that about the army. People had big mouths and loved to gossip. I was so angry that I gave him the silent treatment for a few days and left him without a car.

During that time, some of my coworkers would say I was too good for Bobby or too pretty for him, but that just annoyed me even more. I didn't care what anyone thought and couldn't care less about their opinions. Even though I was angry with him, I loved that man, and nothing was going to change that. I had many missed calls, and Bobby sent me a ton of text messages telling me how sorry and stupid he was. Finally, on the third day, he called my phone, but of course, I didn't answer, so he left a voicemail. He didn't say a word. Instead, Bobby recorded a clip of the song "On Bended Knee" by Boyz II Men. It was little things like that that would make me smile, and once again we were just fine. When I finally talked to him, he told me he couldn't stand the thought of losing me. Bobby said I scared him because he thought I didn't want to be with him anymore and it was killing him inside. I reassured him that was not the case and that I loved him way too much to lose him over something so petty, even though I was pissed about the situation. All was forgiven though, we roughly made up, and we pushed forward together as a couple. Not going to lie, after that, I purposely argued with him from time to time over stupid things just so that we could have makeup sex; it was the best! Terrible, I know. Don't judge me, y'all. I was young!

The next few months were amazing but flew by way too fast. I was definitely not on good terms with Dozier, Rob, and Morgan for a while. Morgan and I had gotten into a couple of arguments and she was practically living with Rob. She ended up pregnant by the Staff Sergeant she was messing with. She was trying to hide it at first because he was married with kids, but everyone in the shop, except Dozier, knew what was going on. She didn't want Dozier to find out because everyone knew she had the biggest mouth.

One day Morgan and I had gotten into an argument in the hallway, and she lunged forward at me and said "What!" like she was going to hit me. I immediately reacted and tried to hit her, but she ran for the stairwell in front of our room, and I ended up pushing her. She tumbled a couple of steps, then got up and ran out of the barracks. I was terrible, I know. Back then, I had a hard time controlling my mouth and my reactions, especially if I felt threatened. I'm not perfect by far and still needed to grow in my maturity. I grew up in a violent household, so I was still in the process of trying to break those bad habits. Morgan was fine, but she cried to Kortney and to Sergeant Goodwin that she was in the early stages of her pregnancy. Sergeant Goodwin called me and told me that we all had to have a meeting at her house. It was stupid. They basically let us yell back and forth at each other insulting one another. Morgan tried to say I slept with someone else, which pissed me off, so I shouted, "That's a lie, but we all know you're fuckin' Staff Sergeant H and you're pregnant by him!" She immediately shut up and started crying, but I was so mad I didn't care. One thing my brother told me early on was that army females tend to have a bad rep, so I had better not be a hoe. People can call me a bitch all they wanted, but they couldn't call me a hoe. Morgan cried and said she didn't want anyone to know. She didn't want anyone to say anything because he was married. Kortney said "Morgan, we all know!" Dozier was the only looking around dumbfounded, and when she realized Morgan didn't want her to know, she promised she wouldn't say anything. I remained close with Kortney but definitely kept my distance from the others. Bobby would let me vent about it but would calm me down and tell me they were not worth get worked up over although he didn't care for them either.

Bobby had a couple guys' nights, and I had a couple girls' nights with Logan, Kortney, and her friend Linda. Linda was a Puerto Rican from New York. She was a military brat who met Kortney when her father was stationed in Georgia. She happened to move out to Colorado with her parents, and Kortney quickly introduced us to her. She was cool. I liked her almost immediately after meeting her.

One night, Bobby asked me if he could go hang out with the boys at their friend Candy's place, and I got upset. I asked him, "Who the hell is Candy?" Bobby said Candy was a guy from his unit, but I didn't believe him. I said "Yeah right! Candy sounds like a stripper name!" He busted up laughing and said I could drop him off just so he could prove it to me. I agreed and the whole way he smiled and joked in anticipation. He said he couldn't wait to prove me wrong and kept laughing. I was like "Okay, we'll see about that. Candy, my ass, what kind of a man was named Candy?" When we got to the apartment complex, he called Candy down, and lo and behold, it really was a guy! Candy was short for Candelaria and Bobby *made sure* to tell Candy that I said his nickname sounded like a stripper name! I was so embarrassed, but we all had a good laugh. Bobby told me that I could always trust him and that we've always been honest with each other so there was no reason to switch it up now. He was right. So I kissed him, and I let him have his boys' night. The whole drive back to post, I kept laughing at myself and smiling at the thought of how excited Bobby was to prove me wrong. I really should've got the hint, but hey, you never know, and I had to make sure. I never had an issue with his boy's nights just as long as he always came home to me, and he always did.

The next boys' night happened to be at his squad leader's house, Corporal Burdios. They told him to bring me along because Burdios' wife, Chris, was going to be there along with Sergeant Thao and his wife, so he did. That night, we ended up taking some shots of Fireball and singing karaoke. It was a good time, but the memory that always stuck with me was when all the guys sang Brooks & Dunn's "Boot Scootin' Boogie" together and "Honky Tonk Badonkadonk" by Trace Adkins. It was a great time. The girls and I just laughed and cheered them on as they sang the songs. Bobby liked country music; he was from Texas after all. He had mentioned that his favorite country song was "Don't Take the Girl" by Tim McGraw because it reminded him of his uncle Johnny who had passed away. His Uncle Johnny used to play the song often, and Bobby grew to love it. He also liked the message of the song and said he finally understood what it meant. I get teary eyed every time I hear it, but I love that song.

One weekend, my cousin Elena invited me to go up to Denver for a family party. I hadn't seen that side of my family since I was in eighth grade when I had lived with them for half a year. I gladly accepted the invitation and asked Bobby if he would join me. Bobby was so excited to go and meet some of my family. He got to meet my Tio Frankie, my Tia Maria, my cousin Elena, and a bunch of other family members at the party. We had a great time, and I remember watching him bop his head to the music. They only played Spanish music that night like rancheras, merengue, and cumbias, but Bobby

48

had enjoyed it and loved the food too. It was so cute to see him get into the music. My family really liked him; he had made a good impression. To this day, they are the only family members who ever got to meet Bobby in person. No one could wipe the smile off his face that night. I cherish that memory and am so thankful for that opportunity.

The week before his deployment, Bobby had gotten a phone call from his best friend Jaime. She had mentioned that his ex, Cheryl, had asked about him, and he told me about it. I loved that we were always so open and honest with each other. Cheryl was Bobby's high school sweetheart but wasn't the last girl he had been in a relationship with prior to me. I understood him because I had experienced the love of a high school sweetheart as well, and it wasn't with my ex either. But in my case, it was with someone who I was very close friends with, Edgar. He was a big part of why I joined the military, but he ended up joining the Marine Corps, and we lost touch. Bobby had actually dated Cheryl, and she was his best guy friend Thaddeus's little sister. That was another thing we had in common. We both had a girl best friend and a guy best friend, and we truly understood each other. Although for first few years of my military career, I had definitely lost touch with my best friend, Rodrigo. Bobby knew Logan was my other best friend, and though he was getting really close to Macias, I had never met his two best friends back home.

Anyway, I asked Bobby how he felt about it, and he said that he cared about her and he wished her well, but that he was happy with me and could see a future with me. He assured me that I was the one who he wanted to be with. But still, I asked him if he was sure. I mean they had history and all, and it was clear that he cared about her. Bobby reassured me, and he said something that really stuck with me even after all these years. I'll never forget his perspective on it. He said something along the lines of "Why leave something great for something that might be greater when that something greater may not turn out to be so great after all? I'm not messing up what I already have, especially when it's already great. I'd lose more than I gain." He used the word *great* a lot, but I understood the message, and it resonated with me. Basically, what I understood from what he was saying is that if you are happy with who you have, you don't want to mess it up with a temptation that might appeal to be "better," but in reality, it may not be better at all. You would lose more than you gain. He wanted me and only me. Bobby made sure that was very clear. I was so in love with this man. He wasn't like any other man I had met before. I was so thankful God placed him in my life, and I felt so lucky to have him. He truly taught me what open communication was all about.

My mom and I were in a bad place most of the time that I was in the relationship with Bobby. She made it clear that she didn't care for Bobby for whatever excuse she had come up with. Her disapproval didn't faze me one bit, but it really hurt Bobby. He had experienced something similar with Cheryl's mom and told me that he didn't want to come between me and my mom. He said, "That just wouldn't be right" and that he would hate himself if he ever came between me and my family. I had to remind him of my past and reassure him that my mom always came up with excuses to push me away. I said, "She doesn't even accept me, and I'm her own daughter!" I reassured Bobby it had nothing to do with him and that it was really just her own issues and her resentment toward me. My dad, on the other hand, didn't mind Bobby as long as I was happy, and he treated me good. My parents had gotten back together at the time and were once again living together.

One day, my parents called me, and Bobby happened to be around. Bobby had the chance to talk with my dad over the phone for a little bit. He told my dad a little bit about himself, told him how much he loved me, and how much I meant to him. My dad was kind to him. He told Bobby all about our crazy family background and told him that I had been through a lot during my childhood. My dad explained that my attitude was bad but that I was a good girl overall and told Bobby just to be good to me and take good care of me. Bobby was so happy after that phone call. It made him feel better that one of my parents accepted him, and that was good enough for him. I was so thankful for that phone call. And it made me feel so good to see Bobby so happy. Family was super important to him, and I absolutely loved that about him. That phone call validated everything that I had told Bobby about my rough upbringing and what I had to experience as a child. It wasn't pretty, and Bobby wanted to ensure that from that point on, I was nothing but happy. He never liked to see me hurting or crying and wanted to make sure he did his best to provide nothing but love, support, and happiness. If you knew my background, you'd truly understand how much that meant to me, but my background requires another book in itself. Bobby really loved me, I knew it, and so did everyone else.

Last Day before Deployment

I'll always regret not being able to spend the entire day with him on his last day stateside. At the time, I was still just a private, and I didn't realize I could have had that day off to spend more time with him. It wasn't until the next day that I found out I could have. That day, I went to work as normal. Bobby had the day off, but he was scrambling to get the last of his things placed in storage. All his electronics, a few clothes, and some hats were placed in Candy's storage. His family never got those items back either, but that's another story. Anyway, after work, he picked me up, and we grabbed a quick dinner. Bobby told me he had to be back at his company for roll call and had to wait there before they could be shipped out. He asked if he could leave a box with me that had a few items he wanted me to hold on to while he was gone. I said of course he could, and he informed me that it was in the trunk of the car and that he would take it up to my room when I went up to change out of uniform. Before he left, he placed his things in my room and then uploaded a music video on to my laptop for the song "Goodbye" by Jagged Edge. He told me to watch and listen to it when he left. I cried so bad watching that darn music video and listening to that song. The music video is about a military man who leaves his family to go off to war. I cried and watched it repeatedly. I love that song. I kept the box in my room for him, but the thought didn't cross my mind to go through the box, so it just sat there in the closet. The plan was that when he got back, he would get his things back from me and the stuff that was in Candy's storage too.

I stayed with him at his company all night. They issued them their weapons, and then we stood around talking and joking with the boys for a while. Eventually it got really late, so we all sat down in the parking lot waiting in their company area. In typical army fashion, we had to hurry up just to sit and wait around for hours, hence the term "hurry up and wait." Bobby asked me again if I would wait for him, and I reassured him that I would. I was devastated that we were going to be separated for a whole year. Hell, he had left for a month just for training, and I was miserable. This deployment was going to be for twelve months, and I was sad that he was leaving me. He kept kissing my face and just kept saying, "Don't cry, ma. I *promise* I'm coming back." (I'm shaking. The tears are flowing just thinking back on it.) Bobby promised me that we were going to start our lives together when he got back, just as long as I could wait for him and remain faithful. I promised him that I was his and only his and that I would wait for him and stay faithful. We waited there so long that I had started falling asleep in his arms. He was sitting against a vehicle, and I sat in between his legs. He had his arms around me and held me tight while I rested my head on his arm. All his friends were seated around and across from us as well.

Next thing I know, someone shouted, "On your feet!" and everyone jumped up. They announced that they were about to head to the terminal and told the soldiers to start saying goodbye to their family members. I started to cry. I wasn't ready for him to leave me yet. Bobby hugged me so tight and said, "I promise I'm coming home to you, ma. I'll be back don't worry." (There is a huge lump in my throat. This is so hard to reflect on.) I just squeezed him and kissed him and said, "You better! You don't got no choice!" We always jokingly said "You don't got no choice" to each other. I'm pretty sure we picked that up from hanging around Kortney all the time. He laughed, kissed me on the lips and forehead, and then said to me, "Besides, I always dreamed that I was going to die in a plane crash. Don't worry, I'm gonna be just fine." Yeah! Like that made me feel any better!

He was about to board a freaking plane! I slapped his arm and said that's not funny. He laughed, kissed me again on my lips and forehead, and then turned and walked away. I had no idea that would be the last time I would ever get to spend time with Bobby, the last time I would ever see him alive. I remember his smile as he waved goodbye and then turned and walked away. I was a mess, along with other family members and wives of the other soldiers who were crying and saying goodbye. I still cry like a baby when I think back on it. (I'm literally crying as I'm writing this.) He was alive, and he was beautiful and still full of life that day. I knew he was sad; I could see it in his eyes, but he remained the strong one for me that night.

I hate that our last moments together were cut short, and I will always regret the fact that I didn't take enough pictures of us throughout our time together. I can never relive that day. I can never get any more time with him, but if I had the chance to redo it, I would've taken the day off. I would have hugged him, kissed him, and told him how much I loved him over and over. Bobby said he knew how much I loved him and claimed to love me even more. I'm not sure if he ever truly knew just how much he impacted my life, just how much I love and adored him, or just how much he meant to me. Only God truly knows my heart and how deeply in love I was with Bobby. The image of him walking away and looking back to smile and wave is vision forever burned into my memory, one that I cherish but that hurts to recall upon, the last time I would ever physically see my fiancé alive.

Just like that, Bobby was gone. I didn't know it at the time, but I'd never see him alive again. It hurts so much thinking about it. I'd give anything to be in his arms one last time. To hear his laugh, to see his smile, to feel his tender kiss or the warmth of his body. I drove myself back to my barracks and cried like a baby the whole way. When I got up to my room, I was uncontrollably and loudly crying, like bad. It was so bad that I accidentally woke up my roommate and scared the crap out of her because she thought something bad had happened to me. It had, the love of my life was just deployed, but I mean I was safe and all, unlike she was thinking. She pounded on my room door, asking me what happened and if I was okay. I couldn't make out much to her but managed to say that I was okay.

The next day, I was depressed and unmotivated to do anything at all. My senior leader, Sergeant First Class Austin, noticed the change, pulled me to the side of the office, and asked me what was wrong. I told her Bobby had deployed the night before. My roommate inter-jected from the other side of the room and told her I scared the crap out of her when I came in crying. She said she didn't know what to do, but that the way I had cried had really scared her. Sergeant First Class Austin hugged me and consoled me for a second (literally, for like a second), but then she yelled at me and said, "Soriano, you should've said something! I would've given you the day off." Ugh, my freaking heart sank. I was heartbroken, upset, and angry when I heard that. I had never experienced anything like that before, so I honestly didn't know. I was so upset that I didn't get extra time with Bobby when I could have. A couple days went by, and I talked to another leader in my shop, Staff Sergeant Ramos. She told me about deployment cycles and made me aware that when Bobby returned, I'd be deploying to Iraq with my unit or would already be out there by the time he got back. I didn't want to be separated even longer, so she recommended that we get on the same deployment cycle.

The only way to get on the same deployment cycle was to vol-unteer to deploy with his unit. It would have to be a permanent move to his brigade, but we would be on the same deployment cycle from that point on. I immediately volunteered to deploy without any hesitation or second thought. Staff Sergeant Ramos helped me with the process. She had a friend named Staff Sergeant Ocampo who worked in Bobby's Brigade S1 (HR department), and they pulled some strings to get me reassigned to that Brigade S1 shop. They needed Soldiers because some of the females were getting pregnant to get out of the deployment.

The best part was that Logan worked in that same Brigade S1 office! I'd be working with her, and we'd be reunited again! We got the paperwork together, and I got to meet Staff Sergeant Ocampo in per-son right before he deployed along with Logan and most of the shop. I was temporarily placed on rear detachment until I could complete deployment training, get placed on a manifest, and get on a plane to Afghanistan. While I was on rear detachment, I got moved into their unit barracks and was working alongside two Army Specialists. One girl was named Moody, and the other was Lopez. They were both pretty cool but couldn't deploy for medical reasons. Moody had just

55

found out that she was pregnant, and the father was Bailey! Bobby's friend! Moody was my barracks roommate, and she was pretty cool. They weren't going to make her leave the barracks until she was further along in her pregnancy. Moody was from Mississippi, was country as hell, and she had a thick accent, just like Bailey. She gave me the 411 on the people in the shop. She told me who was cool and warned me of who I should stay away from or watch myself in front of. She told me that Lopez, Logan, and Johnson were all cool and that I'd get along well with them. She didn't realize that I had known Logan since basic training, but I soaked in the information that she gave me.

I ended up driving the Impala home and left it with my mom. I let my family know I was deploying and was able to say a quick goodbye before I deployed to Afghanistan. Bobby called me when he could by using a calling card that they gave him. It felt so good to hear his voice again, and I let him know what I had done in regard to volunteering to deploy. He was excited at the thought that we would be deployed together. I told him that I must really love him because I literally just volunteered to deploy to war for him. He laughed and told me how much he appreciated me. He said I was too good to him. I loved him; it was as simple as that. I still can't believe I volunteered to go to war for love, but to me, it was worth it, and I would have done it all over again for him in a heartbeat.

A couple weeks later, during the first week of June, it was my turn to deploy! Unfortunately, we didn't find out until later when I got out there that we would be nowhere near each other during our deployment.

Deployment

My departure was nowhere near the same. I didn't have family or friends come to see me off. Moody and Lopez were there because they were part of the process of getting people on manifests and out on to the plane. I also met a couple people who I conducted deployment training with Sergeant First Class Garms and Specialist Quiles. I really looked up to Sergeant First Class Garms being that she had taken me under her wing during training. She wasn't mean, and she actually cared about my wellbeing, which showed through her actions. My first day of training, I was unaware we needed to bring our water source, so I was unprepared. She realized I had no water and had me drink from her camel pack. A camel pack is a bag of water you carry on your back and drink water by sucking through a long tube. It's kind of gross looking back on it, but we didn't care. She just made sure I was staying hydrated. Both Sergeant First Class Garms and Specialist Quiles were flying downrange to Afghanistan with me, which I was thankful for because I wouldn't be alone. When I boarded the plane, I got nervous. The reality set in, this was really happening! I was on a plane that was headed to Afghanistan. Honestly, I felt a little scared, and I was nervous. I knew that I had 100 percent volunteered to do this for the love of my life and didn't regret it, but I mean this was Afghanistan in 2009. Shit was scary and no joke, yet I was going, and there was no turning back. So I sucked it up, got myself in check, said a prayer, and before I knew it, we were off.

We had a couple of stops along the way. My favorite was our layover in Ireland. I had never seen so many shades of green in my life. The land was beautiful, and we could only see what was around the airport! I'm sure there is much more beauty to see there, and one day I'll take a trip back. Next, we stopped at Manas Air Force Base located in Kyrgyzstan, which I had never heard of in my life. (Yeah, I don't remember learning about that country in geography.) Our last stop before I reached my actual Forward Operating Base (FOB) was in Bagram. That base was huge! It felt more like a normal base than anything. We even saluted officers who walked down Disney, one of the main streets on the base. You typically won't salute on the smaller FOBs and Combat Out Posts (COP) being that it places a target on the officer if ever seen by the enemy. Anyway, I got stuck there for a few days and was separated from Sergeant First Class Garms and Specialist Quiles being that they got pushed forward before me. I was able to catch a helicopter which first made a supply drop at FOB Mehtar Lam, so we (me and the other passengers) got off there for 20 minutes and then continued on. Eventually, I made it to FOB Fenty and was reunited with Logan! Staff Sergeant Ocampo was there, and I got to meet Johnson and all the other people in the shop as well.

When I first got there, it was hot. It was like stepping into a dry sauna but not being able to take a break and step out for fresh air if needed. The wind felt like someone placing the hot air of a blow dryer in your face, and sometimes there would be particles of sand that blew all over. We always had to wear eye protection whenever we stepped outside. There were big stacks of Hesco barriers with barbed wire at the tops that surrounded the perimeter of the FOB. I could hear military aircraft flying in and out of the landing strip and the loud grumbling of military trucks coming on and going off the base. There were also sounds of connexes being opened and closed with the faint sounds of chatter from every direction; the base stayed busy. As we got closer to the building we worked in, I could hear the sound of weights being dropped from the small gym and the grunts of the soldiers pushing themselves past their limits. The sounds that I really disliked were the sounds of the jingle trucks and the Muslim prayer songs. They both creeped me out, and the thought of them still makes me cringe.

In Afghanistan, you will hear Muslim prayer songs throughout the day that sound like they are screaming in Pashtu over a loud microphone. They also have these trucks the size of dump trucks or bigger that are colorful with hanging articles and chimes that jingle as they drive by. Those trucks always scared the crap out of me. I was warned about the trucks being used as Vehicle Borne Improvised Explosive Devises (VBIED)—in other words, a huge bomb. There would always be a few that would drive past as we conducted clean up or other details, and I'd always be on edge. People would always share stories about their experiences with jingle trucks, and they were not pleasant experiences, so I was literally scared of those trucks.

Aside from the trucks, we were also warned of the use of dead animals being that the carcass could be used to hide bombs as well. Essentially, the enemy could and would place a bomb in the carcass of an animal, especially dogs, and plant it somewhere alongside of a road to detonate as troops went by. We did see dogs and even monkeys around the FOB. Some belonged to the Afghan National Army (ANA) including the monkeys, but there were also military working dogs that we would see from time to time. The smell of Afghanistan was terrible, but I got used to it. It would either smell of old garbage, the nasty smell of burnt sewage from the burn pits, or of old dirt (yes, dirt has a smell). I could also smell the musty scent of sweaty uniforms and gear whenever I was outside around a group of other soldiers. After a while, I just got used to it. But anyone of those smells can trigger a memory and take me right back to the middle of the dessert or the sandbox as we called it. We also had to learn some of their customs. For example, it is disrespectful to reach out with your left hand when shaking hands with an Afghani. They said that the left hand was used to wipe their butts after using the restroom, so it was disrespectful or rude to them if you offered your left hand to shake. Afghani men were often seen holding hands walking in conversation, being that it was customary for them to do so. And of course, we could not signal the American okay hand sign because that was like flipping the bird to an Afghani and could get you killed. We were taught to always be cognizant of the different customs and courtesies in other countries.

In the beginning of our deployment, I had no way of contacting Bobby via telephone and vice versa. I had to rely on e-mail and

Yahoo Messenger to communicate with him. At the time, he couldn't always communicate, and it was extremely frustrating. The process of deployment and communication can be complicated. It didn't help that he was an infantryman. At the time, I didn't fully grasp the concept of what that meant. I later realized that his job meant that he was placed on the frontline. He would be fighting the enemy first-hand. I was so naive. Even then, it never even dawned on me that I would lose him. I was so stuck on his dream about dying in a plane. Bobby had made it safely, so I didn't even give it a second thought.

Anyway, we struggled to communicate throughout the first few months of our deployment. We went as long as nineteen days without talking at all. To some who are more experienced with deployments, that may sound like nothing, but to me, it was terrible. The lack of communication took a toll on our relationship. We argued a lot over e-mail, but it was mostly out of frustration because we could hardly communicate, and he could not get to a phone to call me. I bought an Afghani cell phone, like everyone else in my shop did, and I also had access to an office phone. At the time, I didn't fully understand what it was like for Bobby. Looking back, I feel like an idiot. At the time, I didn't understand how different our conditions and experiences were. I take full responsibility for all our stupid arguments. His deployment conditions were very different from mine, but I hadn't realized it yet. I was located on FOB Fenty in the northeast, and he was located way down south at FOB Ramrod. Eventually Bobby relocated as his unit helped build COP Wilson, which ultimately expanded and became FOB Wilson. Bobby had moved around and of course was always out on missions. Meanwhile I worked in an office. We had internet and working telephones, which we needed for our job. He used to tease me and call me a POG, person other than grunt. A grunt is the army slang for an infantryman.

The only time we went out to work outside the office was for mail call or details. We had to pick up mail and take it to a connex to deliver mail to the soldiers in our brigade or distribute mail to our sub-ordinate units. Most of the time, we drove our Brigade Commander Colonel George's up-armored truck to pick up and deliver mail over to the connex. There were a few times where I had to drive a right-sided stick shift truck. Sergeant Tejeda and I went each time, and I'd drive because she couldn't drive a stick. Mind you, I had only drove a stick shift car a couple times before, when my friends in high school taught me how to drive one. But since no one else knew how to drive a stick shift, that was good enough! Sergeant Tejeda would just crack up because at first the truck would shake and jerk us forward. I had to get used to the clutch again. She would just bust out laughing, and so would I but not before cussing out the truck of course. Like it was the truck's fault or something. That dang truck was a right-side drive, so it was even more complicated. That was the first time I had ever drove on the right side of any vehicle before. It was weird, and it didn't help that it was a stick shift. All the other vehicles were normal and automatic. We'd always get stuck with that truck because no one wanted to drive the dang thing, so it was always available. Eventually I got the hang of it, and we did the dang thing!

Sergeant Krueger had showed me the ropes on conducting mail operations. I had the task of driving to pick up mail every day up until I got my license revoked. Afterward Logan or someone else with a license had to drive me to pick up mail. They would help me download the truck and then leave me in the mail connex to conduct mail operations. The mail connex was literally hot as hell. Long story short, I was driving Colonel George's up-armored truck and went to pick up mail with Logan. There were a bunch of people there for mail pick up that day. The area was crowded with vehicles and trailers. There was a guy named Ramos who was a reserve soldier who worked at the post office, and he was signaling for me and Logan to park in front of a trailer. He said he would ground guide, so Logan stayed in the truck. I'm sure the military people who read this are going to recognize the obvious mistakes but bear with me.

Ramos stood directly behind the truck and started to ground guide me. I started backing up in front of the trailer and was only going like two to three miles per hour or so because it was only a couple meters away from the truck. Next thing I know, I couldn't see Ramos, but my dumbass didn't stop. (Y'all, I was a private. Don't come for me!) Next thing I heard was loud banging on the back of the truck, and the faint sound of someone screaming to stop. We couldn't roll the windows down in that truck, so I couldn't really hear him well. I immediately stopped and realized I had squished Ramos! Someone else signaled for me to move the truck forward so I hurried up, pulled forward, and parked the truck. Poor Ramos, his leg got pinned between the truck and the trailer. I felt so bad! I jumped out of the truck, and I kept apologizing, but he brushed me off and limped inside. I shouldn't laugh, but I'm laughing thinking back on it! Ramos was okay, y'all! I hurt his leg, but I think it was only bruised up or something. I don't know the full details.

Anyway, his NCO had called back to my office because Ramos went to the medics to get checked out. Sergeant Krueger, of all fucking people, answered the phone. (Just a quick background on Sergeant Krueger, she was an older lady from somewhere in bumfudged Wisconsin, and she was extremely high-strung!) So his NCO told her what happened, and by the time we got back to the office, she had everyone freaked the hell out. She made it seem like I was going one hundred miles per hour and ran over Ramos and he was in the medical treatment facility with his leg cut off or some something. I got in so much trouble and had my license revoked immediately. (At least for FOB Fenty because they had me driving again later in Bagram!) I tried to convince Staff Sergeant Ocampo and Sergeant Wang that it wasn't as bad as she made it out to be, but they didn't believe me until they seen him dancing at salsa night later that week, which they had just started up. Ramos forgave me but gave me crap for it the rest of the deployment. Poor guy, he was just fine though, I swear!

Believe it or not, later in my career, I became a Master Driver and instructed many others on how to drive military vehicles (Lord help them!). From then on, the NCOs would just help pick up mail and dip out while I waited in the humid connex for the subordinate units to come pick up their mail. Our uniforms were long sleeves jackets and pants along with our required gear, which was our weapon, eye pro, the Improved Outer Tactical Vest (IOTV) and our Kevlar (helmet). I never sweat so much in my life. I felt sweat in places sweat shouldn't be in. The worse part was feeling the sweat drip down my back. I'd get drenched in sweat and then have to go back to the office all wet, stinky, and nasty! I shouldn't complain, but it was the grossest feeling having my uniform stick to my body. Deodorant alone was no match for the connex!

The best part about running the mail room was meeting people outside the shop. It was cool meeting new people who worked in other sections of our brigade and within our subordinate unit S1 shops. I got the chance to put faces to some of the people I had to work with over the phone, which was pretty cool. I got to know Specialist Wang, who was a skinny Chinese girl with a thick accent and a big ass gun. She always carried a SAW M249 being that it was her assigned weapon. I don't know she ended up being assigned that weapon. She was tiny, but she rocked it, and it was awesome. There were also people I worked with in our outlining subordinate units. I didn't get to meet most of them face-to-face until after deployment due to our geographic locations. My favorite people to talk to and work with over the phone were Sergeant First Class Robinson who was in charge of the S1 in Bobby's Battalion, Staff Sergeant Cedeno who was in charge of the S1 for 2-12 IN BN, Specialist Ferguson (Ferg) who worked for Staff Sergeant Cedeno, and Sergeant First Class Coulter who was in charge of the Special Troops Battalion.

One time, I had the opportunity to visit FOB Finley Shields where Sergeant First Class Coulter and Specialist Wang were located. It was close enough that they would come visit our shop from time to time. Staff Sergeant Cedeno and Specialist Ferg had come down to our FOB once prior to our redeployment, so I was also able to meet them in person before we got back stateside. They all were funny and really cool to work with, but Sergeant First Class Robinson was my favorite. He was hilarious, and his voice was awesome. He was a very country, older guy from Alabama who legit talked like Major Payne! (Y'all ever seen the movie?) I loved it! Especially when we were on the phone and he'd call someone in the background a turd! It was awesome. They called me all the time to report casualties or ask me to walk them through how to do something in Deployed Theater Accountability System (DTAS), which was one the army systems that we used out there. I quickly became really proficient in my job, and I really appreciated the confidence that they all had in me. I was eventually awarded a coin of excellence by General Stanley McChrystal for all the support that I provided to the brigade.

One of the things we had to do that only made partial sense to me was the cleanup detail ran by Command Sergeant Major Parks. He was in charge of the Brigade Support Battalion. Picking up trash around the FOB made sense. I get it, they didn't want trash everywhere. What didn't make sense to me was how Command Sergeant Major Parks expected us to take five-minute showers but then wanted us to water down a stone memorial that was alongside the airstrip to make it look nice. Seriously? Let's be real here. This was a stone memorial beside an airstrip with dust and sand blowing every single day. Each morning, he wanted us to sweep it, then to waste the water on it for area beautification. After being placed on that detail for the first time, I said screw the five-minute rule and took my time in the shower. Details always sucked, but hey, at least I got out of the office for a few hours. Speaking of showers, one of the worst shower experiences I had was when our water bungalow showers broke down, and I had to take a water bottle shower. You would have thought that the water would still be hot after being out in the sun all day, but nope, I was mistaken. That must have been during the winter months. I grabbed a few bottles from a case outside. When I opened them to shower with, the water was still cold. Not the best feeling at night. It reminded me of the cold showers I used to take in high school, but hey, a shower was a shower. I was grateful to at least have some sort of alternative.

I loved working with Logan. It was comforting knowing she was out there with me. I mean this girl had literally experienced everything with me since day one of boot camp. That was rare. Most people were separated right after basic training, and if not, for sure after AIT. Nevertheless, we were lucky enough to be working together in the same office. We didn't always have the same hours, but we were always lucky enough to at least work a few hours together each day. We hardly got any mail, unless it was something we ordered for ourselves online. Unfortunately, we didn't have family members or friends back home who would send us letters. In fact, my parents and I were once again not on talking terms. My mom threatened to throw all my stuff out of her storage and gave me a week to get it out despite the fact that I was in Afghanistan. I called back to Staff Sergeant Ramos, and she had two guys drive down to Vegas in a U-Haul and pick up my belongings from my parents. Then she had my things stored at her friend's house in Colorado Springs being that they were gearing up to deploy to Iraq again. It was a mess and was really messed up that my mom did that to me during my deployment.

Staff Sergeant Ocampo signed Logan and I up for the Soldiers' Angels and Adopt-a-Soldier programs. They were programs where people back home in the States would send us letters and care packages. Two people impacted me the most from those programs. A single mother named Aimee Collison whose young daughter Alyssa was always excited to receive mail from "her Soldier" and Mrs. Terry Choate. Terry received my name from the organization by chance, but I believe God made that happen. Her son Scott was in the Air Force and just so happened to be on the same deployment and worked in the same exact building as me because he was attached to my unit. How crazy is that?

One day, Scott came in and asked me if I had gotten any mail from a Terry or Theresa Choate, and I confusingly said no. He said, "Well, that's my mother. She got your name from Soldier's Angels, and you should be receiving a letter from her soon!" A couple days later, I received my first care package, and it was from her. We were pen pals the entire remainder of the deployment. We got to know each other well within the first few letters that we sent to each other, and I became very comfortable writing to her. I would vent to her about anything and everything, and she would always write back with great advice. Aimee and Terrie really kept me going; they encouraged me often and helped kept me sane. It sucked watching other people get mail from loved ones, but I began to look forward to their letters and packages which remained consistent throughout the remainder of the deployment. Aside from them, the only mail I got was from Bobby when we would write letters to each other. Terrie is a wonderful person and became like a second mother to me. We had the opportunity to meet a few months after we all returned from deployment. To this day, I call Scott my brother while Terry and her husband, Dave, embrace me as their "adopted" daughter.

Tracking Casualties

When I first got out to Afghanistan, they had me working in the Personnel Readiness Management (PRM) section which was responsible for manning. That meant I had to provide the numbers to the brigade command team so that they knew how many personnel we needed to fill or back fill throughout the deployment. We also worked alongside the medics and operations team in the Tactical Operations Center (TOC) in order to track casualties. Working in the TOC was cool because it was a secure room filled with a bunch of people and we could see live attacks taking place on a big screen. As 9-line MEDEVACS came in, I'd gather the information from either Captain Allen or Sergeant First Class Hesson and start the casualty packets. I would track the casualties until they could be returned to duty or shipped out of Afghanistan for treatment. I quickly learned the reality of war, and my first few Killed in Action packets were difficult to process. The NCO in charge of me was Sergeant Wang, a strong-willed Hispanic woman who was in her mid-thirties and was from San Antonio, Texas. She was very stern and honestly scared the living hell out of me, but I grew to respect her. I admired her work ethic. She was straightforward and mean in a sense that she didn't take crap from anyone. She kept me on a tight leash to ensure I always respected her authority. You never wanted to get on her bad side, which I did a couple times. It was hard to bite my tongue when we pissed each other off because we both had type A personalities, and neither one of us kissed ass. She would bark orders at me when she was pissed, and her facial expressions were the worst. I would just respond with a stern "Roger" and keep it moving until she calmed down and got over her mood swings, but we got through it.

Anyway, Sergeant Wang gave me a pep talk about casualties and informed me of the harsh reality that we would be losing soldiers throughout the deployment. She said while it was very heartbreaking to read the details of the reports we received, we still had a job to do. Our job was to ensure we got as much information as we could about each incident and injuries the casualty sustained so that we could report it up to the casualty assistance office. She told me that I couldn't take it personal or let it get to me because there would be no way that I could survive the deployment if I did. She also said she knew that I had thick-enough skin to handle it and was confident I could be accustomed to our job. I very quickly got accustomed to the process and the importance of our job. It was sad, but the mission had to go on. I followed through with my part to ensure that casualties were appropriately tracked and that we accurately tracked the number of people on the battlefield.

I worked dayshift with Sergeant Wang. Sergeant Lamping, another NCO in our section, worked the nightshift. We would have a changeover brief with Sergeant Lamping every morning when we came in and every evening when we left for the day. We worked twelve- to thirteen-hour shifts depending on what was going on. Majority of the time, it was a twelve-hour shift, so that we had time to conduct PT, which we did on our own. A big part of our job was to take numbers from the DTAS system and plug it into formulas in Microsoft Excel. We used Microsoft Excel for tracking purposes as well. I'm so thankful for that experience. I learned a lot about Microsoft Excel that year and got really good at my job, which paid off throughout the remainder of my career. We did PT after work. Being that Bobby wanted to eat out the entire month before his deployment, I had gotten fat and had a lot of weight to lose. I was determined to lose it too! I wanted to look good for Bobby when we got back stateside, so I worked very hard on my fitness and lost a lot of weight. Besides, it kept me busy, which made the time go by fast.

There was only one Missing in Action (MIA) packet that we had to notate and track, which was for none other than Bergdahl.

His unit was attached to ours as a subcomponent of our Task Force (TF). We were TF Mountain Warrior, 4th Infantry Brigade Combat Team. Sergeant Wang received the initial report and briefed me on it so that I could change his status in the system. It was reported that Bergdahl left his weapon and belongings on the FOB and then simply walked off into the night. How the hell that was even possible, I have no idea. But he successfully got off the FOB and wondered off on his own. He deserted his unit and was later caught by the Taliban as we all know. I'll never forget it because he was our only MIA person, and of course, his story later became a huge ordeal in the news media. I still can't believe he put himself in that position nor can I believe that people actually considered him to be a hero. In my eyes, he was a coward plain and simple.

The hardest situation I had to track casualties for was for COP Keating, which is now known as the Battle of Kamdesh. It was the most casualties we had in one instance, and I felt overwhelmed. As a team, Sergeant Wang and I got through it, and of course Sergeant Lamping as well once she came in. The morning of October 3, 2009, over three hundred Taliban attacked COP Keating from the mountains and eventually breached the gate. It was a roughly fourteen-hour battle that resulted in seven soldiers being Killed in Action, one who Died of Wounds (DOW), and about twenty-seven more who were wounded. It was daunting as all the reports came flooding through. It started off with two or three and then became back to back nonstop. I had to run back and forth between the TOC and the office for information as it came in while Sergeant Wang was on the phone with the S1 Non-Commissioned Officer in Charge (NCOIC) getting updates from him.

Based on the situation report (SITREP), not only had the Taliban attacked but their own ANA (Afghan National Army), counterparts had turned on them as well. The enemy had basically taken out the whole platoon located on that COP at the time. They called for air support and fought as best as they could until the air support finally arrived. The air support bombed the area, which killed most of the Taliban and forced the rest to retreat. Unfortunately, the air support took a long time to get there. If I remember correctly, the air support was coming from our FOB. Due to the distance between locations, it was at least forty minutes before the air support could even arrive from the time the request was sent up. Due to the lack of support and lack of troops on ground, they were outnumbered by the enemy and sustained a lot of casualties. The amount of casualty packets we received that day was overwhelming. Reading the details on the reports and piecing together the event that took place broke my heart. However, I remained focused and did my part to track and report the casualties to higher.

Sergeant Wang and I stayed late that night, and I believe Sergeant Lamping even came in early to help. To this day, I can still remember most of the names of the casualties that took place. I remember a lot of the details from the wounds that were reported on the casualty reports. I especially remember those who suffered severe wounds or had received shrapnel in abnormal areas of their body compared to most. I earned the Mountain Warrior Hero of the Month award for my support with that incident and a couple of other incidences we had to track. It was an Army Achievement Medal awarded each month to brigade soldiers who stood out or did something above average. Honestly, I didn't feel like I deserved it. I felt like I was only doing what I had to do on my end. I simply did my job. The real heroes were those on the battlefield that day.

After that incident, I was scared for Bobby. I told him that he had better be careful and that he and the boys had better take good care of each other. I was worried, especially since I started to see more casualties come in from their unit for different incidents. Bobby reassured me that he was doing the best he could to stay safe and that I was all he was looking forward to after the deployment. Nevertheless, any time that a casualty was reported from Alpha Company, 1-12th Infantry Battalion (Red Warriors), I'd get a little scared. Sadly, but honestly, I was always relieved that his name was never on any of the reports that I had received while I served in that position.

One of the coolest experiences I had out there was attending a shura. I went with Staff Sergeant Ocampo and a group of others from my shop. Our command team organized a shura with either local Afghanis or ANA, I don't quite remember. I just remember sitting in a large circle while our command team sat down with Afghanis and talked over food and chai. We sat on little rugs and ate things like grapes, rice, some kind of meat, and of course, naan. The chai we had in Afghanistan was the best chai tea I've ever had. I don't know what it was about it, but it was amazing! We also had the opportunity to try a cinnamon naan, which we only got a couple times, but it was delicious! I was thankful for the opportunity to experience a little more of the Afghani culture, a side that was different from just the war.

During deployment, communication with Bobby was rough, but we made it work. Bobby and I would e-mail each other, and sometimes, he would call me on my office phone. I'd have to go back in at night to take his calls. We also sent handwritten letters to each other because sending mail to each other was free out there. I also sent him care packages because they didn't have much where he was, and we had a tiny shoppette (store). It was a connex that they turned into a shoppette that sold basic toiletry items, magazines, snacks, tobacco products, socks, and PT uniforms. It was small, but at least we had one. After the COP Keating incident, we were asked if we could donate anything at all to the soldiers who survived because they literally lost everything. Their things were all obliterated during the battle. Logan and I, along with a few others, went to that shoppette and bought a bunch of items like PT uniforms, socks, and toiletry items to send out to them. It felt good to help in some sort of way.

In the letters and e-mails, Bobby would express how much he loved me. He would tell me how badly he missed me and how aside from his family, I was the one thing he was looking forward to most when we got back. He said I kept him going and that he couldn't wait to have me in his arms again. Then one day, he asked me how I felt about having children with him. I was caught off guard, but I was all for it! There was no one else I'd rather start a family with. He was the love of my life. I told him I wanted to do a few things like go white water rafting, snowboarding, and checkout Six Flags before I got pregnant though. I also I told him that I wanted to get married before we had kids, and at first, it made him sweat. But eventually, I received a handwritten letter from him, and in it, he had asked me to marry him. I was ecstatic! I was literally on cloud nine, and my whole shop knew about it! I quickly wrote back and accepted his proposal, but the best part was getting a phone call from him, hearing him ask me about it and being able to answer him over the phone. I already wore on the promise ring he gave me, but it felt amazing to call him my fiancé! I told anyone and everyone who would listen that I had a fiancé!

We talked about having kids all the time after that. I wanted four kids, and he was all for it but mentioned that he wanted a boy first. The deployment had really made him think a lot, and he wanted a boy to carry on his name. I promised him that I would give him as many kids as he wanted, and I meant it until he jokingly said he wanted twenty-seven, the number he wore on his high school football jersey. My parents weren't too thrilled; they thought we were too young. Yet I believed that there was no one in the world who was going to keep me from marrying this man and starting a family with him.

Sergeant Wang got my hopes up by telling me that she was going to FOB Wilson where Bobby was and that I might be able to go as well. Unfortunately, I wasn't able to go because she said they needed someone to cover dayshift while she was gone. Instead, Sergeant First Class Hesson was going with her. I was upset because we all knew she was hooking up with him, and they were both married at the time. I felt like they were just taking advantage of the situation to get extra alone time together. Then again quite a few people we worked with were cheating on their spouses including a corporal in our shop whose husband was a Soldier on rear detachment. That corporal and I couldn't stand each other, and the whole shop knew it. At least I liked Sergeant First Class Hesson. The first dude Sergeant Wang was messing with was a complete jerk and had some serious anger issues. His name was Sergeant Payne, and he yelled at me once just for looking at him as he walked into the shop. I couldn't hide my facial expression that day and fought myself to bite my tongue, but Staff Sergeant Ocampo pulled him aside and corrected him. Nevertheless, I was thankful that Sergeant Wang agreed to take some letters and a package I had for Bobby. She was the only one in our shop who got to meet Bobby in person.

Shortly after, Lopez had been sent out to Afghanistan, so they moved me to awards, and she took over my position. I no longer worked for Sergeant Wang and was placed on a swing shift from midnight to noon. I worked directly under Sergeant Tejeda instead. Sergeant T was a wonderful NCO, and I was thankful that she was a barrier instead of having to work directly under Sergeant Krueger. Sergeant Krueger was in charge of the Personnel Service Support (PSS) side of our shop. I didn't hate Sergeant Krueger, but I disliked how she conducted herself. For example, one time I received casualties, and she tried to ask me if I would tell her who they were. Sergeant Wang was very clear that we were not to reveal any names until the families were properly notified. It did not matter who asked—we could not reveal the names. So when Sergeant Krueger asked me, I told her I couldn't say who it was, and she said, "So what, you think you're better than me or something?" Like seriously? I told her no, and she must've seen the expression on my face because she just said, "Never mind" and went back to her work. I don't know if I had more of a confused facial expression or one of disgust, but I lost respect for her that day. Thank God I reported directly to Sergeant T when I was placed in awards.

Being that we couldn't see each other, Bobby and I started planning our leave together; he wanted to take me home to officially meet his family. He gave me his mom's number and his sisters' numbers as well. Bobby asked me to start calling them and getting to know them, so I did. The phone calls seemed to go well, and I was excited for the trip we were planning to the Texas coast. I made sure that I requested my leave for the same time in March, the time that he had put in for his leave. As the time got closer and closer, we were getting excited and talking about all our plans together. I always say, had we gotten that vacation together, I probably would've gotten pregnant. I know for certain we would've enjoyed every moment together. Unfortunately, things didn't go as planned.

On February 12, 2010, I received the last e-mail that I would ever receive from Bobby. He told me he was glad to hear that his family and I were getting along well. He said that needed to happen if we were ever going to work. He also talked about his sister Angela, who he claimed was going to be the hardest for me to be accepted by. I had told him in the previous e-mail that we talked and laughed over the phone. He said, "Angela has her good days and bad days, believe me, but she can be a good girl, but an asshole too. I guess that's why I'm used to you so much. They prepare me for the worst in females, believe me." I know I had a bad attitude at times, and at times, I was hard on Bobby, but he loved me through every difficult moment. Every up and down we experienced, he was patient and always reminded me of the love he felt for me. I was thankful that there were way more ups than downs and that the bad days never lasted very long. In that e-mail, Bobby mentioned wanting to ensure that we got our own room at the hotel his mom was reserving for all of us at the coast. He told me to tell his family he loved them and missed them. I had more access to phones than he did, so sometimes, he'd ask me to pass a message to his sister Paula or his Mama Peggy.

He wrote, "Tell them all I love em very much and miss them as well… Baby, I miss you so much, it's ridiculous. It's not just sexual, believe me. I miss your beautiful smile, your laugh, and my favorite, your eyes. When I look into them, I swear, I feel like everything is pretty much perfect, and if we were together forever, I'm sorry to say but even though our bodies will get older, your eyes will always look as beautiful as the first day I looked into em. So gorgeous. I miss holding you at night and even acting like a girl myself and letting you hold me, kinda gay. And, of course, you forcing me to hold you because I'm cold at night and need something to keep me warm because you steal all the covers. *Yes, you do.* Can't wait to get home, mami. It's gonna be much wanted and needed leave for me. I am not praying for anything as much as I am for leave. Well, baby, I gotta go. Love you more than you understand. Can't wait for leave."

Bobby always had a way of making me laugh. He always said something funny when he wrote me or talked to me, even when he was being mushy. I wrote him back that evening, but he never had the chance to read my e-mail because he was out on a patrol. On February 13, 2010, my life changed forever.

The Worst News of My Life

I try not to think of this day, but I remember it vividly. I worked a swing shift, which started when I changed over into the awards section. I was working at my desk listening to music on my headphones but had it playing low. Sergeant Lamping got a call saying Alpha Company, 1-12th Infantry Battalion had received casualties. I looked up but kept working. Then she received the reports. The look on her face said it all. I knew right then and there something was wrong. I just didn't know what it was. Sergeant Lamping looked straight at me probably not realizing it, but it triggered my thoughts, and my worst nightmare came to mind. I remember she went straight into Major Fluck's office, and was whispering to her. I just knew something was wrong. I could sense it, but I kept working and tried to think positive. I tried to focus on the music. I was listening to "Cruisin'" by Smokey Robinson. Thoughts kept running through my head. Maybe Bobby only got hurt, but he was okay. He *had* to be okay.

I got up and went to out to the hallway where they kept bottles of water. I grabbed a bottle of water, and when I stepped back into the office, I seen Sergeant Lamping whispering to Sergeant Tejeda. That to me confirmed Bobby's name had to be on one of the reports that came in. I watched as Sergeant Lamping pulled out the casualty folders; there were three red folders and two blue folders. A red folder meant a soldier was very severely injured or worse KIA. A blue folder meant a soldier was injured but not in critical condition. I started praying in my head while trying to maintain my composure.

I prayed to God that Bobby had a blue folder and not a red folder. In my head, I begged God, *Please, PLEASE, God, let it be a blue folder.*

Then Staff Sergeant Ocampo, Sergeant Lamping, and Sergeant Krueger all went into the major's office, and I knew it had to be bad because they didn't ever tell Sergeant Kreuger anything! She was high-strung and had nothing to do with casualties or that side of the office, but she was in charge of me and Sergeant Tejeda. They were whispering so I couldn't hear anything being said. I got scared. I went to the bathroom trying to fight off the tears. And when I walked back into the office, they all looked at me in a way they never had before, but they remained silent. I'm sure they could see the worry and concern all over my face, yet not a word was said. I had to try hard to fight back the tears. I tried to focus on the lyrics of the song. By then, it had switched to "You Really Got a Hold of Me," another song by Smokey Robinson.

I sent Logan a text on my little Afghani phone. I told her something was wrong and that I think Bobby got hurt. I told her everyone in the shop was acting different but that no one was saying anything. No one would tell me anything! I guess they had called Logan as well and asked her to get me out of the office. She was told Bobby was a casualty but was also threatened not to tell me because his family needed to be notified and that I needed to be distracted until they figured out what to do. Of course I had no clue what was going on. Logan arrived at the office, and my NCOs let me off like normal. I was confused and couldn't shake the feeling that something was terribly wrong. I went to the DFAC with Logan to grab food, which was typically my dinner. I was feeling scared and was overwhelmed with anxiety. I couldn't eat. I told her everything that had happened in the office. She reassured me by telling me to stay positive, that Bobby was okay, and to keep my head up. I almost broke down in the DFAC. I told Logan I don't know what I would do if I ever lost Bobby. She said, "Don't think like that, Soriano. Think positive," but I knew something wasn't right. Logan never really called me Soriano. She called me Riano, which was a small detail I caught. She did as she was told and kept quiet about the situation. It took years for her to tell me the truth about that day. She struggled with the guilt, but I don't hold it against her. I understand the pressure and the situation that she was placed in. It was unfair to her, but in a sense, it worked. It kept me distracted.

After I left the DFAC, I got back to my room, changed into PTs (my workout uniform), and looked at the pictures of Bobby that I had taped up on my wall. I started crying. I begged God to let him only be injured. I was fighting my own thoughts, trying my best to stay positive. I yelled at myself out loud, "NO! *He is OKAY, he HAS to be. HE PROMISED ME!*" Then, I heard a knock on my door... I pulled myself together and opened the door. It was Sergeant Tejeda. She said they needed me at the office. My heart started to race, and tears welled up in my eyes. I asked, "Do you know why?" She just said no and tried not to make eye contact with me. I knew she was lying to me. I don't blame her, but I tried to get it out of her anyway. I locked eyes with her and pleaded, "*Please*, Sergeant T, are you sure you don't know anything?" She kept a straight face and said she was sure. That was the longest walk back to the office.

I kept my head down, eyes on the dirt-road fighting back the tears with each dreadful step. It felt like miles, and my body felt like lead. We both remained silent on the walk back, and my thoughts were scrambling trying to figure out what happened to Bobby. I was scared, but I had hope for the simple fact that they let me leave the office without telling me anything. Maybe he was just injured. I hoped he was just injured. I could live with that. I would love him no matter what, and I'd be there for him regardless of the situation. We took the backway to the office. Sergeant Tejeda punched in the code to the security box and held the door open for me. The back corridor felt so long as we walked down the hallway. My heart was pumping so fiercely I could feel the pulse in my throat, and I was shaking the whole time. When I turned the corner, I seen Staff Sergeant Ocampo to the right, standing outside of Command Sergeant Major Sasser's office by the door. He reached for my hand, and I couldn't hold it in anymore. The tears started flowing, and all I could muster out was his name. As if I was pleading, I softly said, "Sergeant Ocampo," but he just pointed to an empty room across from him and led me in. Major Fluck was sitting inside on a brown leather couch against the wall. When I saw her, I knew it was bad. It had to be something bad. They told me to sit down on a chair next to the table. I did as I was told, but I could not stop shaking.

Command Sergeant Major Sasser walked in with Chaplain Madej. Command Sergeant Major Sasser sat down in the chair in front of me and grabbed my right hand and placed it on the table. He looked me in the eyes and asked me, "Is Specialist Bobby Pagan your fiancé?" I started sobbing, and through the lump in my throat, I softly answered, "Yes, Sergeant Major." He then stated, "I am so sorry. Specialist Bobby Justin Pagan was Killed in Action while out on patrol…"

I didn't hear the rest, I blacked out for a second, and the rest of his words were drowned out by my scream. I screamed at the top of my lungs "*NOOOOOOO!*" I screamed and screamed, and I uncontrollably wept. I looked to my left where Staff Sergeant Ocampo was seated on the couch, and I grabbed his arms, *begging* him, "*Sergeant Ocampo, PLEASE NOOOO!*"

His eyes teared up, and he just hugged me. Command Sergeant Major Sasser, Major Fluck, and the chaplain all reached for me, but I screamed, "*Noooo, I want Logan!!*" So Staff Sergeant Ocampo ran and got her. I just kept crying and screamed, "*Noooo, my baby!!! Whhhhhyyyyy?!?! Please, God! Whhhhyyyy?!!!*"

Then Logan ran in with her arms spread wide open ready to embrace me. I jumped up from the chair and *clung* to her. I screamed, "*Logan, my baby!! They killed my baby!!!*" I was bawling at that point. I cried like I have never cried before, and she started crying too (which was rare). She softly said, "I know, Soriano. Everything is going to be okay." I just kept screaming "Noooooo!" in between breaths and sobs. Chaplain Madej attempted to talk to me to try to calm me down, but I wasn't having it. At that moment, I no longer wanted to hear what anyone had to say. Logan just held me as I cried into her chest. Her uniform top was soaked in my tears. (I literally relived this moment as I wrote this. I had to stop several times. I'm bawling, but I had to let this out.) Command Sergeant Major Sasser then told me that Bobby's family had not been notified yet, so I couldn't call anyone or tell anyone anything until they were notified. I was still sobbing, but I mustered out, okay.

Command Sergeant Major Sasser said they were going to treat the situation as if we were married and send me back to the States bright and early the next morning for emergency leave. He also mentioned that I had to remain in my room until his family was notified. Logan stayed with me the whole twelve hours that I was held in my room. I believe Sergeant Tejeda and my roommate Rainey were there as well. All I wanted to do was cry and sleep so that I could wake up and this could all be just a bad dream. I wanted everything to go back to normal, but this terrible nightmare was real. Logan packed my clothes for me. She stuffed some clothes into an assault pack for me so I wouldn't have to do anything. I literally couldn't do anything but sob. I was numb yet in so much pain all at the same time. My heart was shattered, and I was broken. I was in complete and utter shock. I hugged and held tightly on to a longhorn's cotton stuffed hand that Bobby had sent me in a package. I kept looking at Bobby's pictures and rereading his handwritten letters that he had sent to me. I cried and cried. I begged God to give him back to me. I cried out to God, *"Why? What did I do wrong?"* I begged, pleaded, and apologized to God for whatever I did, over and over.

Finally, they confirmed that Bobby's mom had been notified. I had my Afghani cell phone on me, so I immediately called my older brother right there in my room, and I broke down again over the phone. I don't know what made me call my brother first, probably because I subconsciously always looked up to my older brother. I knew he understood the harsh reality of war being that he too was a soldier. As kids, I'd turn to my older brother for protection and comfort whenever our parents were fighting, and I think I just needed to hear his voice in that moment. His voice was comforting to me. I remember my brother said, "Aww, I am so sorry, sis. I am so sorry." He comforted me as best he could but ultimately suggested that I call my mom. My mom and I were not on the best of terms, but I called her anyway. She told me how sorry she was for my loss, asked me a few questions, and ended the call by telling me to keep my head up.

When I was finally allowed out of my room, we went straight to the office. I immediately called Bobby's mother, Peggy. I started crying right when I heard her voice. She was crying too. She asked me if they were sure that it was Bobby. I said yes. They confirmed it's Bobby. We both cried over the phone. I told her I still had hope that they were wrong. Earlier that year, there was an incident with multiple casualties, and a family was notified that they lost their loved one. But that particular soldier turned out to be okay because there was a mix-up with the names. I prayed to God that was the case, but unfortunately, it wasn't. Peggy and I cried and cried on the phone, and then Bobby's older brother Robert grabbed the phone and asked what happened. I told him what I knew and tried my best to comfort him. When he passed the phone back to Peggy, I let her know that I would still be going to Texas and would be leaving soon. Turns out another family was notified as well because they got Bobby mixed up with another soldier named Bobby Pagan and eventually apologized for the mix-up.

The whole trip back to the United States, I was alone. I honestly just kept crying silently each step of the way. People looked at me but didn't really question me or bother me, and I was somewhat grateful for it. I just could not stop the tears from flowing. I could not sleep at all, and I didn't want to eat, but I forced myself to eat once in Kuwait. Bobby mentioned that he wanted McDonalds when we got home. I wanted Olive Garden, and he wanted McDonalds. There happened to be a little McDonald's stand in Kuwait, so I forced myself to eat some for Bobby. Honestly I couldn't really hold it down. I was literally sick to my stomach. I tried to eat a little bit for Bobby, but I couldn't stop crying. I made sure to call Peggy and check up on her and ask how the family was holding up. I made a promise to Bobby that I would stay strong for his family, especially for his mom, and I tried really hard to stay strong for them while I was there. I really did.

Meeting Bobby's Family

When I landed in Austin, I didn't have a phone that worked anymore so I went up to a payphone in the airport and called Peggy. She told me that the girls (Bobby's sisters) were at the airport looking for me. Ana and Paula came in and found me at the payphone. I recognized Ana from seeing her pictures, but I confused Paula with Angela. The girls just looked at each other when I greeted them, but they didn't correct me. I had caught my own mistake though. I had never met Bobby's family before. I never had the chance to, so my first time meeting them was tragic, and together we had to lay my fiancé to rest.

Bobby has three brothers and four sisters; I met all the girls first. The girls drove me back to Mama Peggy's house where she was speaking to the casualty assistance officer. When I finally got to meet her, she was so kind and embraced me. I fought back every tear that I could and tried to remain strong. She was trying to be strong too, but I could see the pain in her eyes. She was heartbroken as well. When I spent the first night there, I slept on the living room couch. It was weird being in the house that Bobby grew up in without him. As I lay there on the couch with the TV on, the back door slowly opened. Chills ran down my spine, and I got creeped out. I worked up the courage to get up and shut the door. If I hadn't gotten much sleep before, I certainly didn't get any that night.

After that night, I slept on the floor in Ana's room. Throughout the time that I was there, Ana was back and forth from a friend's house, so at times, she would let me sleep on the bed. When she got back home, she'd take my place on the floor. I appreciated the nights when she would stay up with me and talk about Bobby. She would share her memories of him with me, and I'd share some memories that I had with her. Thinking back on memories always made me feel better, especially the memories that would make me laugh. If there is one thing Bobby taught me, it is that laughter is good for the soul. However, when I was alone in the bathroom or when everyone was asleep at night, I would let it out and sob as quietly as I possibly could. I had to cry into my pillow a few times in attempt to keep anyone from hearing me. I tried my best to maintain my composure and remain strong for Bobby and for his family, especially for Mama Peggy.

Bobby's Funeral

Bobby's older brother Robert went to Dover and accompanied Bobby's body back to Texas. That day was extremely hard for me. We stood there and watched as the plane landed and pulled up on the runway next to us. When they pulled out his casket, I completely lost it and broke down in tears. I could not hold it in any longer. In that moment, I could not be strong. My body went limp. Mama Peggy held me close, and I cried and cried into her chest as she held me tight and tried to comfort me. I couldn't breathe. I just sobbed and sobbed literally until I ran out of tears and was heaving short gasps of air. Mama Peggy's shirt was soaked. At the end of my breakdown, she tried wiping my hair out of my face and the tears out of my eyes, but there were none left. They had all soaked into her shirt. It hurt my soul to see that casket come off that plane. That was the first time I got to meet Robert, and it is a memory that I will never ever forget. They told us how badly Bobby had been hurt and suggested a closed-casket funeral service. There is no way I would have ever had closure with a closed casket. We were told that Bobby's skull was messed up from the blast. He was killed by a suicide bomber on a motorcycle. As he drove by their platoon, he detonated himself killing three soldiers and wounding others. The casualty assistance officer also told us that the right side of Bobby's body was injured, which physically affected the appearance of his arms, stomach, and leg. I just cried. How could they hurt him so badly?! Bobby was a wonderful person, yet they hurt him so bad. I was angry! Bobby happened to be giving candy to some local Afghani children when that suicide bomber drove by and took his life. Bobby died rendering an act of kindness. The love of my life was doing what he did best, showing kindness and bringing smiles to others. It killed me inside that this was happening. I could not believe it, yet I was going through all the motions. This was really happening. This was real.

They took Bobby's body to a funeral home so that Mama Peggy could see his body. Bobby and I never married, so they only let Mama Peggy and Robert back to see his body. It killed me. I *had* to see him. I could not bury him without physically seeing him. There was just no way. When Mama came back out, she was in tears. She said he looked good and that the funeral staff were going to help fix him up so that he could have an open casket funeral. I was so relieved. My mom flew down for his funeral. I was shocked but so grateful that she came to support me during that time. I finally felt like I mattered to my mom. I truly appreciated the fact that she took the time to fly down to Austin to be with me during my time of need. Despite our issues and despite how she felt about Bobby, she was there for me and even paid her respects to Bobby. Her support meant the world to me.

I finally got to see Bobby's body during the viewing in the funeral home. I went up to the casket and just looked at him. I observed every inch of his body that I could possibly see. The first thing I noticed was that he had a white paper-mache type of wrapping around his neck. I'm sure they tried to hide it, but I could see it popping up from under the collar of his uniform. I wasn't sure if that wrap was supposed to help cover his wounds or help hold that area together. His skull was sunk in on the right side, so his beret didn't fit properly. Bobby's face was swollen, yet he was recognizable. There was no doubt. It was definitely my fiancé lying in that casket. I couldn't see a difference in his arms, legs, or stomach because he was covered by his military uniform. They did a really good job of cleaning him up even though I thought they put a ton of makeup on his face. I'm sure it was probably to help cover up his wounds and bruising.

The vision of Bobby as he lay in the casket with his hands clamped together across his stomach is forever etched in my memory. He wore a fresh Class A uniform with his updated award ribbons and badges, white gloves, and shiny black army shoes. I am personally scared of dead bodies. Hell, I couldn't even get near my grandma's ashes. But in that moment with Bobby, I didn't care. I held is hand, I hugged him, and I kissed him. The warmth of his touch was absent. Instead, his body felt ice-cold. I wept. I promised to be forever his, and I said goodbye to the love of my life. I then sat back down and bawled like a baby. I was thankful for the time everyone let me have at his casket. That funeral home was full, but I was able to have my moment with him, and I know I took a while. I was very grateful for that. We later had his funeral service at a Catholic church down the street from where Bobby grew up. I don't remember much about the service to be quite honest. I wasn't mentally present, only physically there. I do remember Ms. Karma, a friend of his family, singing "It's So Hard to Say Goodbye to Yesterday" from the floor above us as everyone exited the church. It was the song his family had chosen for him. To this day, I cannot listen to that song without crying.

Mama Peggy decided not to have Bobby buried in a military cemetery because the closest one was an hour away. Instead, she opted to have him buried at Assumption Cemetery close to home. Because of that, she was not going to be provided with a military headstone, and the expenses fell on her to cover. She had a nice personalized headstone created for him etched with the army seal, the symbol of his beloved longhorns, and picture of him in uniform on it. She also had his casket encased with a burnt orange lid that had a silver plate on top. Etched on the silver plate was a huge burnt orange long horns symbol on the left and the US Army seal on the right. His name and years lived were etched on the bottom right beneath the seal. It was beautiful.

When we buried him, I was numb. I don't remember anything that was said. I just remember the folding of the flag, them handing the flag to his mother, and the gunshots from the 21-gun salute. I just held it all in and was focused on his casket. Was this reality? I felt insane. I was physically present and going through the motions, but mentally, I was checked out, questioning whether or not this was really happening to me. When they started to lower him into the ground, the tears started flowing, but I cried silently. As the crowd started to disperse, I just stood there watching his casket being lowered into the ground. I was frozen; I could not move. I silently stared in shock and disbelief. They were burying my soul mate, the love of my life. Bobby was no longer alive to continue our journey.

My mom stuck around with me but stood back and gave me my space. After a few minutes, she walked up and said, "Come on, *mija*." We had to go back to the church hall for his reception. I wanted so badly to hug my mom and cry. I wanted her to hold me and tell me everything was going to be alright, but I couldn't. She was the person who used to call me weak when I cried, and we honestly weren't very close. I wasn't sure how she'd react. I didn't want to risk upsetting her, so once again, I held it in. I just looked down at his casket and said my final goodbye to my other half. I knew that when he had died, a part of me died right along with him. He took a piece of my heart that will forever be his. I was broken. My soul hurt. I yearned for him, but he couldn't make it all better like he used to whenever I was going through something. He couldn't comfort me and never again would I be held in his arms. My life changed forever. After the funeral, Paula said she was getting a tattoo of Bobby. I told her I wanted to get a memorial tattoo for him as well, so we did. I got a tattoo of the memorial stand with the helmet, rifle, and boots on the outer portion of my right calf with the words "In Loving Memory" above it and "Bobby J Pagan" below it. To this day, it is my favorite and most meaningful tattoo.

Shortly after, we were all invited to fly to Colorado for the memorial ceremony that the brigade was having for him and the two others who died that day. When we got back to Colorado, Kortney met up with me. She hugged me tight, and we both cried. She loved Bobby like a brother, and we all hung out a lot before deployment. She attended the memorial ceremony, and I was so thankful. They conducted the ceremony, and afterward, soldiers walked up and rendered a salute to the memorial stand. I walked up and saluted fighting tears as best as I could before I turned and ran to the bathroom. I had a complete and utter breakdown on the bathroom floor. Kortney came in after me, and so did Chris, Corporal Burdios's wife. They helped me get myself together so that I could go back out for the reception. I truly appreciated them for that.

As my leave came to an end, I was given the option to go back to Afghanistan or return to Fort Carson and remain on the rear detachment. I chose to go back to Afghanistan and finish out my deployment for Bobby. Besides, there was literally nothing left for me in Colorado, so I went back to Afghanistan. I cried the whole way back. I was once again alone and no longer had to be strong. I broke down and let it all out. When I got back to Bagram, I was told I was going to stay there a couple days before I could get on a helicopter to take me back to FOB Fenty. Logan had just returned from her leave and got there a day after me. They housed us in Command Sergeant Major Sasser's empty hooch, which was a wooden building with a queen-size bed and had a TV with AFN (cable network ran by the air force).

Logan asked me how I was doing and asked how everything went with the funeral and Bobby's family. I told her everything. Logan became my sister, my best friend. She was there for me throughout that whole time, and I cherished her for that. I appreciated the bond we shared and was thankful to have her by my side throughout that very difficult time.

Staying Strong, Living On

When we got back to FOB Fenty, everyone in our headquarters knew. Bobby's picture was on the wall of fallen of heroes right outside our office, and no one really knew what to say to me anymore. I felt like people avoided me for a while, except for Logan and my gym buddy, Wenzel. Logan said that everyone thought I was so strong and couldn't believe that I had chosen to return to Afghanistan. She said people would tell her they don't know how I did it or how I was so strong. I never heard any of that though. I felt like most people avoided me like the plague for a while.

There was a Sergeant named Shuler who provided words of comfort here and there on his way in to work, but most people just kept their distance from me. They placed me at the front of the building to greet the Command Sergeant Major and Brigade Commander Colonel George (now General George). They were both very nice to me. Command Sergeant Major Sasser would ask if I was okay or how I was doing but kept it short. I just took it as people just really didn't know what to say. I mean, what could they say? Nothing was going to change what happened, and there wasn't anything anyone could say to make it better anyway. Regardless, Command Sergeant Major Sasser would always check up on me, and I felt like he genuinely cared. I really appreciated that. Command Sergeant Major Sasser to this day has remained my favorite Command Sergeant Major to work with.

My friends Logan and Wenzel helped me a lot. Wenzel pushed me to let everything out in the gym. He held me accountable for a daily gym session every day after I had met him and then really pushed me after I lost Bobby. He would let me vent and would just listen. I loved that about him; he was such a great listener. After I'd speak on how I felt, he would try to cheer me up. Then he'd push me to work out really hard. Even though it sucked, I always felt better after our workouts. We got pretty close over time, and I really appreciated our friendship, especially because I knew he truly cared and just wanted to make sure I was okay.

On Memorial Day, they hosted a memorial run for all our fallen soldiers. Logan and Wenzel both got up early and ran right alongside me. I appreciated how much Logan and Wenzel really looked after me when I came back. It was hard, I'm not going to lie, and I really struggled to control my emotions after that. Sometimes, I'd be there with my head down fighting back tears. Other times, if someone upset me, I'd just go off. I wasn't an easy person to deal with, to say the least. I'd quickly put anyone in their place if I felt they disrespected me, but in the military, that can easily become a flaw.

I remember arguing with Sergeant Krueger out back one night about who knows what, and Staff Sergeant Ocampo had to come out and put us at ease. I almost got in trouble, but she told him she gave me permission to speak freely. That wasn't the last time I got into it with Sergeant Krueger, but I just wouldn't back down. I know I stressed her out, and I eventually apologized to her. It really wasn't her fault, our personalities were just clashing, and she was trying her best to regain dominance. I even went off on Staff Sergeant Ellington one night outside of the MWR because he disrespected Logan. Point is, I had a bad attitude problem and easily overcame anyone without a backbone. I was honestly only afraid of the strong-willed NCOs who could put me in my place. At the same time, I respected those NCOs the most. I think everyone knew I was just going through it because honestly, they never punished me other than a counseling statement here or there.

Looking back, I know I was wrong for the way I acted, and I honestly think someone should have corrected me or put me in my place. On the other hand, I understand why they didn't. I want to apologize for my behavior back then. I can admit I was out of line at times and should've maintained my bearing. I'm thankful for the patience my leadership had with me despite our differences. It took me awhile to realize just how amazing my leadership in Jalalabad truly was. Sergeant Tejeda, Sergeant Krueger, Sergeant Wang, Staff Sergeant Ocampo, Major Fluck, First Sergeant Burdine, Command Sergeant Major Sasser, and Colonel George, I can never thank you enough for the opportunity I was given to bury Bobby. I am even more thankful for the patience you had for me while I was going through it. I was terrible, yet you allowed me to heal in my own way.

Eventually, our deployment was coming to an end, and our leadership decided to send me and Logan to Bagram to help with the flight manifests and getting people back stateside. They had us give up our rooms for the incoming personnel who were going to replace us. We were placed in a room together but had to sleep on beds that had no mattresses. We legit slept on barbed metal beds for a couple days until we could fly out to Bagram. It was terrible, but I was thankful that they kept us together. In Bagram, we had to work for Master Sergeant Robledo, and that guy really didn't like me for some reason. He was an old Puerto Rican guy who seemed to like Logan but was an asshole to me. One day, he told me that we had a flight line detail where we needed to stand and salute as fallen soldiers were boarded on to the plane. Believe me when I say that I was not ready for that, and it was extremely difficult. But Master Sergeant Robledo couldn't care less if I had just lost my fiancé. I was being placed on that detail and was expected to execute. Logan kept encouraging me, but I literally hated that guy. Master Sergeant Robledo took us out to the flight line but stayed by the vehicle.

As we were walking out to the flight line, Logan and I ran into our drill sergeant from Basic Training, Drill Sergeant Chadwick. The army tends to be a small world at times. It was awesome seeing him, and it helped cheer me up. I mean who the hell runs into their Drill Sergeant downrange in Afghanistan? Me and Logan! I called out to him. He was shocked but totally excited to see us. He asked how we were and asked what was wrong after seeing the distraught on my face. We quickly said hello, told him what we were doing, why it was hard for me, and then said goodbye so that we could complete the mission for the detail. He told me to keep my head up and ran back to his squad. Back then, you could not show emotions; it was very frowned upon. I stood there at the edge of the plane alongside Logan, and we rendered our salute.

Due to the sensitivity of what we were partaking in, it was hard holding back the tears as the caskets with folded flags on top were being carried on to the plane. I got through it, and we headed back to the truck where Master Sergeant Robledo was waiting. I immediately tried to jump in the backseat, but Master Sergeant Robledo locked all the damn doors on the truck. I leaned against the door, lowered my head, and silently let the tears stream down my face.

Logan hugged me and said, "It's okay Raino. You're strong. You did it." Next thing I know, Drill Sergeant Chadwick ran over and yelled at Master Sergeant Robledo to "quit being a dick and open the fuckin' door to the truck!" Master Sergeant Robledo didn't even know what to say. He just looked dumbfounded and unlocked the truck. Drill Sergeant Chadwick gave me a quick hug, told me it was going to be okay, then opened the door and told Logan to look after me. She said that she would, and he quickly left. I will never forget that day. He stood up for me even though I was just a Private First Class, and I respected him so much for it.

Thankfully, there were other people in Bagram who were nice to me and became great mentors. First Sergeant Morris and Sergeant First Class Pippens were two of those people. Sergeant First Class Pippens, or as we called her Mama Pippens, was a lot older and super sweet to us. She tried to get me and Logan to attend the church services with her, but at the time, I refused. I just couldn't. We also started getting people in from the unit replacing us. They were out of Fort Campbell. Some of them were low on ammo and being that Bagram was supposed to be safe, Logan gave away her rounds and was walking around with empty magazines. She said I did too, but I honestly don't remember giving mine away. Then again, a lot of the time after I returned to Afghanistan became a blur.

A couple days later, Logan and I experienced a glimpse of the battle firsthand. We had been mortared before on FOB Fenty, but those never landed very close to us. Eventually we became accustomed to the booming sound and whistling of the incoming mortar rockets. This time, however, we were asleep in our hooch, which is like a wooden hut that had multiple beds in it. Logan and I roomed with two female NCOs who worked in another section of the unit. We woke up to a loud *BOOM, BOOM, BOOM!* It was so close to the hooch that everything in it began to shake, and things were falling over everywhere. All four of us jumped up out of bed and immediately started getting on our boots and gear on. The NCOs in the room got ready before us, and I'll never forget this—they freaking left us.

A Staff Sergeant and Sergeant left behind two Private First Class Soldiers and ran for their lives. Fuckin ridiculous! I got all my gear on faster than Logan probably because I was scared shitless, and the adrenaline had kicked in. She was struggling to get her Kevlar on. Her hands were trembling, so I attached the clasp for her. We grabbed our weapons and ran. The mortar rounds had not stopped the entire time, and the blasts were close as hell. As we ran, I could hear the buzz of the bullets fly by from the small arms fire behind us. I still remember seeing little rocks and dust pop up from the ground around us where the rounds landed as we ran. The wooden buildings around us were set up in what seemed like corridors, but there were a lot of open spaces between them. We ran as fast as we could to the closest bunker that we could find. That was the scariest shit I ever experienced in my life!

Logan was faster and ran ahead of me, but I tailed right behind her. I didn't dare slow down or look back. I kept up, and we just kept running until we finally reached a bunker. The bunker that we found was full of navy personnel. There were no army soldiers around us whatsoever. The attack lasted about an hour or so, but it felt like forever. Logan and I looked at each other. We were both teary eyed, but we remained silent and soaked it all in. I realized I had my little Afghani cell phone in a pouch connected to my vest, so I quickly sent a text to my mother telling her that we were being attacked and that I loved her. Yeah, my mom freaked out after that, especially being that I didn't reply until it was all over and done with. When my brother found out about that, he got upset. But the way I seen it was that Bobby didn't get a chance to say goodbye to his mama. Had we died that day, I wanted my mom to know that I loved her.

When the sirens went off for all clear, we got out from the bunker and walked back to our company area for accountability. Master Sergeant Robledo didn't have any accountability of us during that time and seemed relieved to see us, yet he didn't ask us if we were okay. Instead, Master Sergeant Robledo made it clear that despite what had just happened, we were not to submit the paperwork for a Combat Action Badge (CAB). He said he would not allow it. That bastard didn't know what we experienced or if we were even alive for an hour long and yet was already depriving us from a badge we earned. According to Army Regulation, a CAB may be awarded to any non-infantry, non-medical soldiers who personally engaged or are engaged by the enemy. Sergeant Wang had earned her CAB by passing ammo to the gunner when their patrol got attacked by small arms fire. We were two fuckin' privates running through that shit. But he said what he said, and because we were just privates, we couldn't do anything about it. I lost all respect for that man.

Word got back to Staff Sergeant Ocampo about the attack, and he called to check up on us. Staff Sergeant Ocampo was the example of a true leader, and I respected him so much for it. Get this, those two NCOs who left us each got a CAB. I know because I processed the orders for the awards. It was freaking insane to me. I later heard a quote by Matshona Dhiwayo that resonated with me: "A warrior is defined by his scars, not his medals." Some of us have invisible scars, so now, I couldn't care less about the awards. I know what we experienced and survived from that day in Afghanistan.

What occurred was that the enemy used mortar rounds as a distraction while Taliban forces cut open the wire on the back fence closest to our living area. Thankfully, there was a small unit of marines whose living area was right next to the fence where they had broken in. The issue was the Taliban had on army uniforms that they had gotten from the Afghani guy who ran the laundry services on Bagram. The marines were confused by it but quickly reacted as the enemy attacked. We were so close to the area that as the small arms firefight occurred, some of the rounds (bullets) were shooting past us. Air support couldn't help because of the issue with the uniforms. When it was all said and done, the marines left the dead bodies on the fence as a means to intimidate anyone else wanting to attack in that area. All I know is that Logan and I will forever have a bond. We came into the army together, we trained for our jobs together, we deployed together, we almost died together, and we survived together. That type of bond can never be broken.

Redeployment

Eventually, we finished out the deployment and headed back stateside. Logan and I got to fly back with Sergeant Tejeda who met up with us in Manas AFB. We also got to spend some time with Lopez who was placed there to push out soldiers from Manas. We first landed in Bangor, Maine, for a quick layover. It was emotional because there were veterans, and people with flags lined up on each side of the hallway. They were waving flags, clapping, cheering, then shook our hands, and welcomed us home. I felt such an intense sense of pride. *I did it.* I finished my deployment, and I did it for Bobby. I knew he'd be proud of me. After Maine, we flew to Colorado and were yet again welcomed by veterans. They were on the flight line waving flags, clapping, cheering, and welcoming us home. It was a beautiful sight to see. A couple soldiers got off and literally kissed the ground before heading into the building. Redeployment is a very emotional time. Most people are just relieved and happy to be back stateside. Once we got to the building, they handed us water, snacks, and McDonald's cheeseburgers. Then they had us fill out some paperwork. Afterward, they gave us a quick brief about what was about to happen when we got back to the base. There was going to be a redeployment ceremony before soldiers could be reunited with their family and loved ones. The veterans there happened to be veteran riders. They are the veterans who ride on motorcycles and accompany the police in clearing the streets as the soldiers return. We were all placed on buses, and off we were back to Fort Carson. On the way, we were escorted by the local police and veteran riders.

As we got close to post, there were people holding welcome home signs on a bridge above the road. When we downloaded the buses, they placed us in formation so that we could march into the building where families were waiting to be reunited with their soldiers. As we walked in, "American Soldier" by Toby Keith was blasting over the speakers. The crowd in the stands jumped up to their feet, started cheering, and were waving signs in the air welcoming back their loved ones. I have no words to describe the feeling, but trust me when I say that is some emotional shit! I feel a lump in my throat and tears are welling in my eyes just thinking back on it. After that, we stood there at parade rest as they played "Courtesy of the Red, White, and Blue." I never felt so proud in my life.

The commander said a quick speech and we were placed at the position of attention, then ordered to render a salute for the national anthem. I literally had tears flowing down my cheeks and to this day I get emotional whenever I hear the national anthem. It hits different after a deployment and became entirely more meaningful, especially after the loss that I endured. The crowd gave us one last cheer, and then we were released to go run and find our families. That moment was so emotional; there was not a dry eye in the room. However, Logan and I were literally the only two soldiers who did not have family waiting for us there. Not even joking, we were literally the *only two*.

So Logan and I walked out the back door to grab our bags and hop on the bus that was headed to the barracks. She was going to be my roommate! It was kind of sad, though. The bus driver had some boxes of Domino's Pizza waiting in the front seat for *all* the soldiers who were headed to the barracks. Yeah, Logan and I were literally the only two who got on the bus that day. The driver felt so bad he gave us all the pizza. Logan's dad was driving down the following weekend with her car, and at the time, my family couldn't care less about me, so it just was what it was. It felt weird being back, especially being a couple blocks away from Bobby's barracks. Logan and I planned a trip to Hawaii together for block leave because I was supposed to go with Bobby, and neither one of us had been there before. However, we had to complete reintegration training before we could go on block leave.

As people were returning, I found out when Bobby's unit was returning so that Logan and I could attend. Macias and a few of the guys were coming home, and I wanted to be there to welcome them. We sat with Macias's family, and man, let me tell you, the redeployment ceremony is just as emotional from the crowds as it is being a soldier standing on the floor. When Macias came running up to us it was heartwarming and heartbreaking at the same time to see his dad embrace him and just break down in tears. His whole family was crying and hugging him. Then he walked up to me said, "Hey, sis," and gave me the biggest hug. I cried my fucking eyeballs out. Macias was like a brother to Bobby, and so was Bradley. It hurt me so bad to not be able to see Bobby march in or run out to the crowd. Some part of me still hoped to see him, but the reality was I would never, ever, see Bobby again, and that hurt like hell.

Bobby's family had sent me a card with everyone's signature on it welcoming me back home, and it was the sweetest surprise. Candy gave me the 1-12th Infantry Battalion Memorial Coin he received, which was blue with a silver trim and had a soaring silver eagle in the front with the words "Never Forgotten" displayed to the left. The back of the coin displayed all the names of their fallen soldiers along the rim of the coin. The center displayed the dates the soldiers fell with a star representing how many soldiers were lost that day. It is my favorite coin to date, and I have quite a few.

Gone but Never Forgotten

When we got back and I got my stuff settled in my room, I felt like I was losing my mind. Weird things started to happen that scared me at first, but I eventually got used to it. I know I sound crazy, but I swear I would hear my hangers move in my closet where I had Bobby's shirts hanging. Now listen, I am scared of spirits, like seriously, so I legit said out loud, "Bobby, if that's you, I'm glad your checking on me, but I don't want to see you! I don't do spirits, and you know it!" I never physically seen him, thank God, and I was low-key scared when I heard things, but it was cool in a way. I swear it had to have been Bobby. I don't care how crazy I sound, hear me out. My phone would randomly turn on Pandora, and a Jagged Edge song or another song that Bobby loved would play. I'm so serious!

One night I was with Macias and Bradley, and my phone was on his counter, and it did it! "Lost" by Gorilla Zoe started playing out of nowhere. We all looked at each other and said, "That's Pagan!" I said, "See, I'm not crazy. My phone goes off out of nowhere!" One of the times I had went home to visit his family and his gravesite, I swear he was messing with me. I brought him flowers, which I always got from a florist named Helen Rodriguez who worked at H-E-B. She was always there and would put together a dozen red roses with baby's breath like the time he brought it for me. Helen was so kind to me and even offered to deliver flowers to his gravesite for me whenever I couldn't physically be in Austin. January 2018 was the last time I have seen her. Whenever I go to Austin and stop at the H-E-B by Mama Peggy's house, I always look for her; she was heaven-sent.

Anyhow, after picking up flowers for Bobby, I headed to his gravesite at Assumption Cemetery. There was a waterspout close to his grave that had a hose connected to it that people could use to water plants and flowers or whatever. I had grabbed the hose to add water to a vase I bought that was specifically for gravesites because it had a stick at the bottom and could be stuck into the ground. When I turned the water on and grabbed the hose, it sprayed me as if someone had stuck their thumb against the nozzle of the hose. I laughed, but I felt like it was Bobby messing with me. He would do something like that. Every now and again, when I'm at Mama's house, the front door will open by itself, and Angela will just say, "Hey, Bobby!" Then she'll close the door. That stuff still creeps me out, but at least I'm not the only one who sees it happen.

Back in Colorado, I retrieved my things from Staff Sergeant Ramos's friend and thanked her for helping me out. I took it upon myself to go through the box Bobby had left with me. I had his original Class A uniform, the watch he always wore, some more shirts, and I even found a small package with his wisdom teeth in it. I know that sounds really weird, but he had them pulled before deployment, and for some reason, he hung on to them. Don't judge me, but I literally cherished those teeth for years because it was the only physical thing that I had left of him. It wasn't until around 2016 that I finally passed his teeth and everything else off to his mom.

The kicker is when I was going through his items, I found a small baggie with a wedding band. Do you recall when Kortney had told me that there was another ring? I found it! Y'all, I bawled like a baby! I sat there on the floor clinging to the ring in one hand and his teeth in the other, and I cried and cried. I called Kortney and his mama telling them both that I had found it. And of course, I screamed and told Logan! To this day, I have the full ring set and will forever cherish it until the day I die. It is a simple reminder that Bobby is gone but *never* forgotten.

The Mountain Warrior Memorial Ceremony

On June 3, 2010, our unit had a huge memorial ceremony honoring all the fallen soldiers. They invited all the families of the fallen soldiers and had a beautiful ceremony for them. The names of all the soldiers we lost that year are etched in stone and placed in a memorial area right outside of the Fort Carson main gate. Major General Perkins gave a speech and stated, "The greatest tragedy in life is to live your life and not know for sure if you made a difference. The soldiers that we are memorializing here today did not suffer that same fate. They knew from the beginning that their life would make a difference, and it has." He was absolutely right. Bobby had made such a difference, not only in my life but in the lives of many others as well. He impacted so many people both in and out of the military.

The piper then played "Amazing Grace" on the bagpipes, and I swear most of the people in the family member section around me were in tears. Something about the sound of the bagpipes just hits you something fierce, especially after losing someone to war. Then they did roll call. Roll call is when the first sergeant will call out names of people who are present in the crowd, who will then stand up and say, "Here, First Sergeant!" Then the first sergeant will call out the names of the fallen and repeat their name three times after not hearing a response.

When I heard "Specialist Pagan… Specialist Bobby Pagan… Specialist Bobby J. Pagan…" and didn't hear a response, it once again hurt my soul. Just another very real reminder that Bobby was truly gone and there was nothing I could ever do to change it. It was a very hard pill to swallow, and I was not ready to let go. The 21-gun salute was rendered and was immediately followed by taps. At that point, Mama Peggy, Ana, and many others around us were crying. The process was extremely painful. I wasn't ready for closure.

The Healing Process

After deployment, we had mandatory redeployment training and then we were given the option to take block leave in July. I took a trip home for a visit before I went to Hawaii with Logan. My mom had taken over payments for the Impala and was keeping the car for good. It was weird seeing the Impala. She didn't realize it, but the first time we went somewhere, I hesitated to sit inside. When I got in, the car looked completely different. The seats were the same, but the windows were darkly tinted, and she had added in a custom stereo so that entire area looked nothing the same. She also added a small carpet that covered the dash and had her nickname for the car engraved on it. Sitting inside the Impala made me so sad because it looked nothing like it did before. I thought of all the special memories Bobby and I shared together. Things were never going to be the same ever again, and that was a harsh reality to accept.

Once we returned from Hawaii and got settled back into a routine, Logan dated Macias for a while. I hung out with Macias and Bradley a lot on the weekends. We'd just get drinks, and they would tell me about all the things Bobby had told them about me on deployment. Macias was so good to me; he really was like a big brother. I'd get drunk, and he'd let me cry. Then he'd put me in his bed, finish drinking with Bradley, and would sleep on the floor until the next morning. He always looked out for me and told me he got me if I ever needed anything. He felt the need to look out for me. He did it for Bobby and looked after me for quite some time, even after he and Logan split. Not going to lie, it was awesome seeing them together—my best friend and my brother from another mother. It was a great time. We did a lot together like hiking and going to Six Flags. They made me get out because I was really depressed and didn't want to do anything half the time but sleep and hold on to the stuff Bobby left with me. I was drinking a lot as a means to cope with the pain. The only emotion I allowed myself to show was anger. I was great at my job, but I had such a bad attitude and people couldn't tell me anything. I was fierce and ruthless. Logan and others we worked with loved my dominating attitude. They would tell me I was that bitch and no one could say shit to me. Everyone viewed me as this strong person. Honestly though, I was deteriorating inside and was just trying to cover it up. I don't know how I always had access to alcohol. I wasn't twenty-one yet, but I drank a lot during that time.

One day, one of Bobby's friends told me he had something he wanted to give me—a little trinket of some sort for Bobby—and invited me to his barracks to pick it up. His barracks was down the street from ours, so I went. We started talking about Bobby and started drinking. I drank so much that I blacked out. Unfortunately, he took advantage of me. When I came to, he was on top of me, having sex with me, but once again I blacked out. When I came to again, I was naked in the tub full of water. He was on the phone speaking in Spanish telling whoever he was talking to that he was going to hell. He was splashing water on me, trying to get me to wake up. I got up, got my clothes on, and called Logan to come get me. She picked me up, but I didn't tell her what had happened. I didn't tell Macias or Bradley either.

That was the first sexual assault I experienced in the military. I never reported it because I was underage drinking and didn't want to get in trouble. Instead, I blamed myself for putting myself in that situation and for making stupid decisions. It wasn't the last time I was sexually assaulted in the military, there was one more incident later on in my career. However, it was a wake up call to slow down on the drinking. Wenzel had tried to get me to slow down on the drinking as well, and it damaged our friendship. He invited me to a house party he threw, and of course, I drank too much and didn't make a good impression on his wife. She did not like me at all. When I no longer felt welcome, I tried to get my keys and leave, but Wenzel had taken them because I had been drinking. He was being responsible, but I was angry that he wouldn't let me leave.

Another NCO we worked with yelled at me in front of everyone. I was so embarrassed and angry. I wanted to get the heck out of there, so I left without my keys. The problem was my wallet with my money and my military ID were all in my vehicle, which was locked. I called Logan who took his side and told me to stay. I was so mad. It was the only time me and Logan ever got into a serious argument and the same with Wenzel. So I called Ferg crying.

Ferg and his wife came to pick me up, and I crashed at their place for the night. At least I was in a place where I could sleep comfortably. The next morning, Ferg drove me back to Wenzel's, where my vehicle was. Wenzel had left my keys at the bottom of my windshield, and I was pissed because someone could have stolen my vehicle. Logan and I didn't talk for a week or two. Wenzel and I didn't talk for a couple of months. My drinking was becoming a problem, and I started to hate myself. My mom was an alcoholic, and for someone who wanted to be nothing like her, I was surely turning into her. I lied on all the screening questionnaires that are put in place to get us help because of the fact that I was underage. Instead I gave them the answers they wanted to hear. I pretended not to have issues, I maintained the strong fierce persona, but inside, I was crumbling. I stopped drinking and became a hermit again. I stopped going out completely. I was depressed, but at least, I stopped making stupid decisions and salvaged my friendships.

Eventually, I was told by my leadership that I needed to go to behavioral health, which is basically like therapy for soldiers. Back then, there was a huge stigma about behavioral health, and I was scared it would ruin my career. SGT Wang went with me and spoke to the behavioral health counselor. They placed me in a program where I could be seen by a provider off post. I went to therapy, and I wish I could say it helped, but it didn't. Maybe I wasn't open to it, but I was annoyed by the questions the lady asked me more than anything. I was diagnosed with PTSD, Insomnia, and Major Depression. I had mixed feelings about it. Not only was I worried about the stigma, but I was also ashamed because I wasn't strong enough to prevent it.

I was worried about what people would think of me. *I'm supposed to be the strong one.*

Not only that, but some people don't believe that personnel serving in a non-combat arms MOS can experience PTSD, let alone get a valid diagnosis for it! To be honest, people in combat arms often discredit the service and deployments of people who serve in a non-combat MOS. Yet there I was, a *paper pusher* with a diagnosis for PTSD, and I couldn't believe it. Who the hell was going to believe or even understand how a freaking paper pusher can have PTSD? I was ashamed and kept it to myself. I didn't want to rely on prescription drugs to get by either, so I did as best as I could to stay strong and carry on as normal.

There were many evenings where I would take a drive and park across from Commo Hill. I'd hike up to the top and just sit there alone listening to music on my phone. I often played songs like "Just a Dream" by Carrie Underwood, "One Sweet Day" by Mariah Carey, "Missing You" by 1st Lady, and "Dancing in the Sky," the YouTube version sung by Jade Ramos (I now listen to the Beverly Ann Version). I also listened to "I'll Be Missing You" by Diddy, "When I Get Where I'm Going" by Brad Paisley, "This I Promise You" by NSYNC, and of course, "Goodbye" by Jagged Edge. I'd take in the fresh air and watch the sunset before hiking back down and heading back to my room. Something about sitting there with the music playing and feeling the fresh air hit my face just helped me clear my head, and at the time, I really needed that.

I refused to go to church. I'm not going to lie, I seriously questioned God when I lost Bobby. I was angry with God for quite some time, but it was all part of the process. I felt like God took everyone I loved away from me. I was hurt, and I seriously felt unworthy of love. I wallowed in my pain, questioning everything about the life God put me through. I was angry, and I was sick and tired of people saying God does everything for a reason. I couldn't fathom any reason why God wanted me to suffer my whole life. I couldn't understand why God took away the love of my life so soon. I couldn't understand why we just couldn't get those last two weeks of leave together. I had a ton of questions but no answers. I was angry. I was hurt. I was broken.

I truly suffered at night when everything was still, and there was nothing to do or focus on. I had really bad insomnia for quite some time. For the life of me, I just could not sleep. Eventually I gave in and got a prescription for sleeping pills. I believe it was Ambien. I remember having a very vivid dream that I can still picture to this day. I was stuck on it for quite some time. I had dreamed that I was at some party or get-together and Bobby walked in with a group of other soldiers. He walked up to me, grabbed me by the hand, and told me he was home. I cried and hugged him so tightly. I told him, "No, they said you were dead! I buried you." He told me it was all a coverup and that he was working with Special Forces. He said he had been alive all this time. Then he kissed me, and the soldiers were calling him, so he turned and walked away. I was crying, trying to grab him, but I woke up. That dream messed with my head for a while. It was so real, and I struggled with it. I even called his mom and sister Ana and told them about it. Ana shared with me that she had dreamt of him too and said that he must have just been visiting us in our dreams. That dream really got to me though.

A few months after we had returned from Afghanistan, Logan and I were selected to attend an outward-bound retreat alongside other soldiers within our brigade. Looking back, I realize our leadership kept us together a lot. First Sergeant Burdine and Staff Sergeant Ocampo probably had a lot to do with that. They were really great leaders, and I am seriously thankful for their support during that time. It was a free trip, and we thought it was going to be a nice, relaxing vacation. We were seriously mistaken! We were flown into Pensacola, Florida, with First Sergeant Hood who was going to be taking over as our First Sergeant for headquarters and a group of other soldiers. We were driven to Alabama and then placed into two separate groups. It was a great experience, but it was hard work versus a relaxing vacation. We were to paddle twenty miles a day in a canoe along the Mobile River and camp alongside the river each night until we got to our final destination. We also had to carry the food rations we had for the trip along with the toilet, which was basically a large white bucket we had to use. Let me tell you, after returning from Afghanistan, shitting in a bucket for a week straight was not ideal nor was the cleanup, but we made do.

We were given oats to eat each morning that we would fill with water and a little bit of sweetener to turn it into a cereal-type consistency. It was actually pretty good. I didn't mind it. I can't remember everything we had for lunch or dinner, but I do remember rice and getting fresh shrimp one night from a fisherman we ran into along the banks of the river. Now that I think about it, I honestly don't know how he had fresh shrimp being that we were on a riverbed, but it was pretty good.

We got to know our group who consisted of mostly combat arms soldiers. Logan and I were the only two females in our group, so we shared a tent, of course. Each night we had to share stories about our experiences not only on deployment but in life as well. It was pretty apparent that a lot of us experienced loss or hardships. Sharing our stories not only helped us get to know each other better but also built respect and an understanding between us. Each morning, we would pack up camp and start another trek down the river. We got to know Specialist De Jesus and Specialist Agee pretty well because Logan and I did not do well with our first attempt at sharing a canoe. We were each partnered with someone else. I paddled along with Specialist DeJesus, and Logan paddled along with Specialist Agee. We also had the opportunity to see another side of First Sergeant Hood, which was pretty cool. We were given workbooks that we would use to write and reflect at times during the day, typically after lunch or so. Some of the best moments of that trip were getting to swing on a rope swing into the water (even though I failed miserably and hurt my big toe) and jumping into the river throughout the trip to take breaks when it got extra hot out.

One afternoon a bunch of us jumped in, and as we were swimming, someone spotted an alligator. I never swam so fast in my life to get back into the canoe! It was a safe distance away from us, but we did get to paddle by it as we continued our trek down the river. The trip was hard work physically and mentally, although I believe it bonded us together as battle buddies and definitely created cohesion and teamwork between us all. In the end, it was a great trip and overall was a good time.

After outward bound, I was placed in the promotions section, and my new first line NCO was none other than Sergeant Wang! The

Chinese girl with the big gun in Afghanistan. Working for her was tough at first and, to be honest, a little frustrating. Not only was it hard to understand her, but she was very technical about every little thing. I didn't appreciate her leadership style until a few months in. Sergeant Wang wanted to ensure that I fully understood my position and would always have me look up or cite regulations as to why we had to do certain things. She pushed me, but she helped mold me into a great leader. Because of her, I became very proficient in citing regulations, and she pushed me for advancement. Of course, Master Sergeant Robledo didn't want to sign off on me attending warrior leaders course, which was a course needed for career progression. Instead Sergeant Wang took me straight to First Sergeant Hood who knew me from the trip and gladly blessed off on me showing up as a standby student. I got in and served as the student first sergeant for the first three weeks until I failed one of my dang tests and had to retake it. Oh well, I bounced back! Sergeant Wang was a great leader, but she ended up getting married and was sent to Korea with her husband, Magee. We later reunited in Korea and again in Hawaii where she finally became a Warrant Officer, which was seriously well deserved. She was tough on me, but she cared, and I looked up to her not only as a leader but as a mentor.

Anyhow back at Carson, Logan and I were still roommates, and as time passed by, Logan pushed me to try to date because she felt really bad for me and said that I needed to get my mind off it. It was only going on a year later, but I tried. The first guy I dated, I only went out with like two times. The second time, we went to a party that Logan invited me to, and Bailey happened to be there. He pulled me aside and said, "Who the fuck is this?" I told him he was someone I just started dating, and Bailey wasn't having it, not one bit. He was a friend of Bobby's, and I respected him, so after that night, I didn't see that guy anymore.

Later on, I met some guy named B at work and we eventually started dating. At first, I was skeptical about him, but Logan urged me to just live a little, so I continued. What I appreciated most about him was that he had deployed with us and lost friends so he kind of understood the emotions I was dealing with. I didn't know him during deployment, of course. He would always let me vent about Bobby after we understood each other. I won't go into much detail because my relationship with him calls for another book on that alone.

Eventually, I had an opportunity to go down to a line unit to be part of their Battalion S-1.

As a Corporal, I was the first S1 female in my *entire* brigade to work in an infantry battalion S1, down in a line unit as they called it. I was damn proud of that. I set the standard. Shortly after, other S1 females were assigned to some of the other line units in our brigade. Eventually, we got more females in my new S1 shop as well. I was assigned to 2-12th Infantry Battalion which was B's former battalion, go figure. It was an adjustment for the guys, but Staff Sergeant Crowder, Specialist Martin, Specialist Cox, Private First Class Webster, and Sergeant Johnson were all pretty cool. The Battalion S1 NCOIC was none other than Sergeant First Class Robinson, the guy who talked like Major Payne and was formerly in charge of Bobby's Battalion S1! I absolutely *loved* working for him, even when he'd call us all turds!

The guys initially tried to watch their language around me but quickly realized I was worse than some of the guys. I cussed a lot, no doubt, and didn't take no crap from anyone. I was quickly known as the regulation queen. You couldn't get anything past me, but everyone respected me for it, and I frequently got asked for assistance. I loved the confidence my coworkers and superiors had in me. It also felt cool to be the first female in my brigade to go down to a line unit S1 shop. No lie, I felt like a badass, and my confidence exuded it as well.

Before long, we were training up for another deployment to Afghanistan. This time, Logan was gone. She was sent to Germany, and most of the other people who were on my first deployment were either moved to another duty station or got out of the military. So this time around, I took an opportunity to train outside of the S1 shop for a special program, Fort Carson's first ever Female Engagement Team (FET). FET was a team of women who were going to work alongside the infantry on our upcoming deployment back to Afghanistan. Training was spearheaded by Captain DiSilvio who was one of the toughest officers that I have ever worked with, and she needed volunteers for her program. When I found out we would be on the frontlines with the infantry, I gladly volunteered. I wanted payback. I marveled at the thought that there could be even the slightest opportunity that I could get payback for Bobby.

I was certainly out of my element. I wasn't quite as confident as I was back in my shop because we were learning different combat tactics. We were trained by the 10th Special Forces Group and by some of the platoons within our infantry battalions. It was highly competitive, but I made the cut! I volunteered, worked my butt off, and even became a team leader. I was initially assigned to A Company, 2-12th Infantry with Captain Allen who was a medical officer that I worked with in Afghanistan. I impressed the unit I was assigned to by outshooting some of the guys during marksmanship qualification out on the range during a Brigade STX (training/field time). I was a dang good shot and got 39/40 on my marksmanship test. I was determined! I prided myself in having continuously kept up that score up until the day I got out of the military. I loved being able to fire my weapon and watch the targets fall down. I hated paper targets though but only because I was blind as a bat.

Before I got Lasik, it was hard to see. Pop-up targets, on the other hand, were big enough to zone in on, but I'd still always miss one dang shot. Never did get a 40/40, but I was close! I loved the females I got to work with, especially Jessie, Liz, and Evelyn. I was humbled very quickly after joining the team because a good handful of the females could outdo me in running or rucking. Compared to them, I wasn't as good as I thought I was, but I kept pushing myself past my physical and mental barriers. They were some of the baddest females in the army. Some of the best I have ever come across, and I seriously looked up to Captain DiSilvio.

We did a lot of cool stuff like helicopter training, training with paintball guns, firing AK-47s, learning Pashtu, and of course, learning a crap load of different infantry tactics. Training was hard, and I really had to push myself beyond my comfort zones, but it was worth it. I was in the best shape of my life! Unfortunately, my time on FET was cut short because once I got married, I was placed on orders to Korea where B was being sent. However, before I left Fort Carson, I worked up the courage to go back to church. It was a Christian church located at the world prayer center in Colorado Springs. The worship and the sermon literally had me crying in my seat, and I finally turned back to God. Everything the pastor said that day felt like it was directed at me. I knew God had been there all along waiting for me with open arms, but my hurt and anger kept me from turning to Him up until that point. It wouldn't be the only time I turned away and certainly wouldn't be the only time that I sat crying in a church at the mercy of God nestled in his presence. I continued going to that church for a month before I had to make the move to South Korea.

In South Korea, I had another very vivid dream about Bobby, but this time, I was no longer using sleeping pills. In the dream, the scenario was very much the same. I was at some party or get-together of some sort because it was crowded. Bobby walked through the crowd and grabbed my hand, but this time, he said, "You're married now?" I cried and told him that I thought he was dead, and he literally gave me the same story that he was working with Special Forces and that it was all a cover up. I cried and begged him to forgive me. But he simply kissed me, said, "Be happy, I gotta go" and walked away. I woke trying to grab him and stop him from leaving, but this time, I literally woke up with tears in my eyes. Once again, I reached out to his mom and told her and Ana about the dreams. Ana had said it was probably his way of telling me it was okay. I'll never forget it. That dream once again messed with my head, and I struggled in my marriage. I stopped making posts in remembrance of Bobby on social media when I was asked, "How does your husband feel about that?" I asked B how he felt about it, and he said, "Honestly, I thought you would eventually stop but you haven't." I took that as a hint and completely stopped. I once again returned to hiding my emotions.

Two years later, I got pregnant, and in 2014, I gave birth to my son. Bobby's sister Ana told me that she had a dream that Bobby was telling her that my son Cameron was his son and she kept telling him, "No, he's not." I always get emotional talking about these dreams. She said it felt so real, and I knew exactly what she meant by it because the dreams were so vivid. I didn't have another dream about Bobby until I was divorced and living in Hawaii with my then two-year-old son. It was the last dream I had of Bobby to this day. It was very different from the first two. We were alone in a grass meadow with small white and pink flowers surrounding us. In my dream, we got to spend a full day together lying in the grass, talking and laughing like we used to. He kissed me softly and passionately. Once again, he took my breath away. I enjoyed every moment of our time together in the meadow. It was as if no time had passed and things felt normal again, but eventually Bobby stood up and said he had to go. He walked away, slowly letting go of my hand. He turned his head to look back at me and smiled. Then he was gone, and I woke up. It was a beautiful dream, and it felt so real. This time, I woke up smiling, but tears flowed when I realized it was still just a dream. I didn't call anyone that time either. After all, it had been seven years since he passed, and by then, I just kept everything to myself. I haven't had another dream of Bobby since. I miss getting "visits" in my dreams, but I am thankful for the few that I had.

If I'm 100 percent honest, I have not fully healed, and I don't think I ever will. I have learned to cope with what happened and have tried my best to keep on living as best as I can. Clearly, I went through a phase where I relied heavily on alcohol, but there were also times when I seriously contemplated suicide. Depression can be a bitch. I somehow always managed to pull myself out, especially after I had my son. Cameron gave me a reason to keep going, to keep living. I'd be lying if I said I haven't had suicidal thoughts even after Cameron was born. I can say I have fought the thoughts off each time because I know my son is the one person in this world who needs me most and whom I actually matter to. I could never hurt him in that way. I also always made it a point to take off the thirteenth of February each year not only for my own sanity and emotional well-being, but to be able to go through the box of things I had in remembrance of Bobby. I'd sit and read our letters and e-mails to each other, touch all the items that reminded me of him like little gifts or trinkets he had sent me, and then I'd hug his uniform tightly. One day a year, I would allow myself to feel his loss but would never fully break down. I couldn't allow it. I also stopped celebrating Valentine's Day being that it is the day following his death, and I no longer felt the need to celebrate love after such a grave loss. To this day, Valentine's Day is just another day to me, and I don't really care to celebrate it.

Over time, I learned to cope with it and simply hide the pain from others who were wondering why I hadn't been able to "move on" or "just get over it." Yes, people asked that, especially those who served in the military. I somewhat understood their perspective only because back then being emotional in the military was highly frowned upon. You are expected to bounce back and keep moving forward. You can't stay stuck in your emotions; it is not the military lifestyle. The only "accepted" emotion to show was anger, and for me, that was easy to take on and exude. Death just becomes another aspect of the lifestyle and the military culture. I struggled, but I did it.

I kept pushing forward and threw myself into my career. I realized if I could focus my energy and attention on work, I was good. I just had to stay busy so that my mind was occupied. Staying busy has remained my coping method over the years. I hated not having work to do to keep me busy, which made me a prime soldier and a great candidate for leadership positions. I took what I learned from the NCOs that I admired and tried to imitate them throughout my career. However, I meant business and demanded respect. I didn't accept anything less than the best effort from my subordinate soldiers and wasn't ever cool with them until right before I would leave a unit.

To be honest, most of them hated me, but a lot of them looked up to me because I set the example for them. There was nothing that I would ask of them that I wouldn't join in and do alongside them. While I was hard on them, I prided myself in going to bat for them and would stand up for them at any point in time. I really cared about each and every one of the people I was placed in charge of. I wanted the best for them, even if I didn't show it in a manner they expected. I didn't want to be like Sergeant Goodwin. I became a female NCO mashed up from the personalities and work ethic like those of Sergeant First Class Austin, Sergeant Tejeda, and both Sergeant Wangs I had previously worked for. Most of them didn't take crap from anyone. They worked hard, were good at their jobs, were strict, and all of them truly cared about the soldiers who they lead. I may not have been the best NCO and was certainly not the easiest NCO to work for. I'll own that, but I truly cared and prided myself in not repeating what Sergeant Goodwin had done to me. I was a hardass and strict NCO for all except the last two years I served in the army. I was fierce and ruthless but was forced to calm down after I got my first and only field grade Article 15. After that, my fierce personality started to dwindle. Eventually, I lost the fight in me which ultimately lead to me getting out of the military.

I kept myself busy all those years with my career, and when I got out, it was a very difficult transition. I no longer had anything to keep my mind busy. I finally had a huge breakdown in the middle of a casino parking garage. My best friend from high school was able to console me and helped me through it. Rodrigo held me as I poured out my pain. I cried so intensely that he was brought to tears. He embraced me in that parking garage until I was done and could get myself together. He also encouraged me to go back to therapy. I sought help multiple times before in Washington State and in Hawaii before I got out of the army, but nothing had helped. Yet I was once again open to it, so I went to the VA and asked for help. I stuck to one-on-one sessions versus group sessions. I once again informed my therapist that I was against being reliant on prescription drugs but was eventually convinced to try starting with a small dosage. I was issued Zoloft for major depression. Everything that I had stuffed over the years had started to resurface. It was painful to think about losing Bobby, but I also had deeper rooted issues of abandonment that I wasn't ready to face. When Bobby passed, those issues resurfaced, but I stuffed and bottled up the emotions for as long as I could. The problem with that was I could stuff and stuff, but eventually, I would explode, and it was never pretty. I realized that when I don't deal with all my issues and just stuff them down deep inside of me, the beast within slowly starts to force its way out. Yet even after knowing that, it has been a hard habit to shake. Writing has been a saving grace for me. Not only can I keep my mind busy, but I can safely express myself and somehow just let it all out.

I love thinking of the good times we shared, but reality sets in, and it is still hard to face even though I have *accepted* the loss over the years. This is why I no longer believe that it will get better in time because it simply hasn't. I don't cry as much as I used to, but I also hardly discuss what happened. Whenever I go into detail, the memory is vivid, and I relive all the emotions as if it had happened just yesterday. It has been over ten years since I lost Bobby. Yet it is still just as painful, and it hasn't gotten any easier or better over time. Once again, I'm at a point where I am faced with insomnia. It is very difficult for me to get a good night's rest. Writing has helped, and I've been told it is a great tool for healing because I'm getting another chance to let it all out. I have, and while I feel better after a good cry, the pain doesn't cease or lessen. So I'll say this—there are many stages and many aspects of healing. Each person handles loss differently, but I don't think the pain of the loss goes away, at least not in my experience. The pain of losing Bobby is eternally mine. I see it as a grave reminder of just how much I loved him, just how much he meant to me.

Maintaining My Relationship with the Pagan Family

When I met Bobby, I was in a bad place with my family. To this day, I tiptoe around my immediate family members. If I upset them, I can be instantly cut off from their lives, and that always breaks my heart. When I met Bobby, they weren't really talking to me, and we had problems whenever they did talk to me. I told Bobby that I just wanted to feel accepted and loved for once. I wanted to feel like I was part of a family for a change. He always told me that he had a big enough family for the both of us. He wanted to mend every broken part of me and would do anything just to see me happy, laughing, or smiling. He would look into my eyes and see beyond the surface. I couldn't hide anything from him emotionally, but I loved it. I always cried about how I felt about my parents and my older brother. I cried about never feeling accepted or good enough for them, no matter what I did to try to prove myself. Bobby would grab me by the chin, stare deep into my eyes, and say that he loved me and that I was more than good enough for him. He said one day we'd be a family, and it didn't matter what anyone else said or did as long as we had each other. He truly was my prince charming. He showed me love in a way that I had never experienced before. He truly cared about me and my well-being. He mended some of my pain with his overwhelming love, and I can never repay him for that.

Bobby was so excited to take me home to meet his family but didn't get the chance to do so. Bobby's mom and his brothers and sisters meant everything to him. He loved them so much! I adored how excited he'd get to share pictures with me and tell me all about them. Bobby has seven siblings, three brothers and four sisters. Robert, Paula, Jodie, Angela, Ana, Chris, and Miguel. Bobby was a middle child born right before his sister, Angela. As I reflect today, I look back and realize that Bobby gave me a family. The Pagan family has embraced me over the years, and I'm still invited to family parties and holiday celebrations. We have maintained our relationship, and they will forever be my family.

Peggy

I call Peggy "Mama" because she's been like a mother to me. It hurts me to see her cry or to see her sad. At the same time, I love that she can let her emotions out around me because she's always so strong all the time. I love when she opens up to me, but at the same time, it breaks my heart because I can't heal her pain. Bobby loved her so much, he would have never wanted to see her in so much pain. He wanted to make her life easier because he was so grateful for her. Bobby once told me, "Baby, if my momma don't like you, sorry, but you gotta go!" And even though he said it jokingly, I knew he was serious. I reassured him by saying, "Babe, your mama is gonna love me!" I told her about that, and at first, she didn't believe me. She said, "That doesn't sound like something Bobby would say," but he had ended up writing her a letter telling her what he said to me. Mama just laughed and said, "That boy! I can't believe he said that to you." She then admitted that she didn't believe it until she seen it for herself when he wrote her. I loved how much he loved his mama. My mom used to say, "If a man loves and respects his mom, he will do the same for you." She was right.

Bobby held his mother on a pedestal, and it was no secret that Bobby treated me like a princess. He was a gentleman and always treated me with love and respect. I absolutely loved that about him. Mama has grieved in a familiar way. She tries her best to put a smile on for everyone and essentially cries alone to herself. Sometimes, when Bobby is mentioned or brought up, she'll tear up or cry a little bit, but she quickly recovers. She keeps her mind busy at all times.

Like me, she threw herself into her work and has kept up with two to three jobs working everyday almost all day. She is one of the strongest people that I know. I have so much love and respect for her. I just wish there were something that I could do to make her feel better. Anything to help brighten her day, but I feel powerless. A mother should never have to bury her child. Mama has been deeply scarred by the loss of her son, but an onlooker would never know it because she conceals her pain so well. I admire her strength and her courage. I cherish my relationship with her not only because of the relationship we've built but because Bobby adored her. She was the single most important person in his life. She is my mama, and I will always love her as such.

Robert

Robert is Bobby's older brother. He is the only one I never really felt accepted by. Bobby only told me a little bit about Robert prior to us meeting. Robert was a big reason why Bobby joined the army. Bobby told me that after Robert left, he felt like he had to step up as a man and take care of his family. Over time, Robert spent less and less time visiting his family. It upset Bobby, but he still wanted to follow in his big brother's footsteps, so he joined the army. The difference was, Bobby made it a point to go home and visit his family as often as he could. Bobby went home at least twice before deployment to spend time with his family. The last visit was completely last minute, but he wanted to surprise them. He was so excited to come back and show me pictures of all of them. When we lost Bobby, I talked to Robert on the phone from Afghanistan, and he asked me a few questions about his little brother. I let him know that Bobby looked up to him because he did. Robert told me he never got to see Bobby in uniform. He was kind to me when we met in person but was standoffish. Mama told me that his wife at the time, Alison, had gotten to his head. Robert didn't believe Bobby and I were engaged because he never mentioned it to him. Touché, but Bobby also hardly talked to Robert at the time. He talked more to his mom and other siblings in Austin. Mama told me that when she got Bobby's stuff back from

Afghanistan, there was a letter addressed to her that he never got the chance to send. In the letter he mentioned me and told her that he wanted to marry me. She showed the letter to Robert, and she told me that he believed it afterward.

Unfortunately, things have always remained kind of awkward between us. The issue was that Alison's younger sister, Whitney, had a thing for Bobby. I found out because I broke into Bobby's e-mail. I knew all the answers to his recovery questions, so I was able to change his password and get in. I saw that Bobby and Whitney had e-mailed each other a few times because they were in his sent folder. After he passed, I met Whitney in person. I also seen that she had sent Bobby an e-mail stating that she didn't know what he seen in me and that she had hoped that they would have gotten married and had kids one day. I literally laughed! No way in hell would that have ever happened, sweetheart. Bobby was mine and I was his. Nothing and nobody would've ever come between us. Alison also wrote Bobby an e-mail saying that Whitney was heartbroken, that she had looked forward to his messages, and that she missed him. Shortly after reading all that crap, I deactivated Bobby's e-mail account.

When Robert deployed, I made sure I was there in Texas right alongside his family to see him off. Since then, Robert has remarried and has had three beautiful children. I think his new wife, Angie, is way better than his ex, but I could be slightly biased. I drove six hours from South Carolina to Alabama where he lived to see Mama and Angela who were visiting him at the time and to meet his little family. It was still a little awkward, and I had my son with me. But it was nice to see him after all these years. Now, they are back in Texas and I've seen them at a couple of family parties. It's still awkward, but I hope over time it gets better. Robert and I will probably never be close, but he is Bobby's older brother, so regardless, I will always love him as a brother for that simple reason.

Paula

I really clicked with Paula from the very beginning. I would call her from Afghanistan at Bobby's request, and we would talk for a couple of hours. She shared stories about Bobby's childhood, and I would just laugh. She was helping us plan our trip to the Texas coast, and I remember Mama asking if we wanted one big room for all of us or two rooms. Bobby told me to tell Paula to make sure me and him got our own room because we needed alone time. I remember telling Paula and just laughing over it because he had called and told her as well. She's older than him so she understood exactly what he meant. She told him, "Don't worry, I got you, bro!" When I was there in Austin for the funeral, I was always with Paula and Ana. I felt close to her and loved how open she was with me. When I got back to Colorado from Afghanistan, I literally drove twelve hours to Texas on every single three-day or four-day weekend that we had, which was just an extended weekend off. I wanted to spend every moment that I could with them because they were all I had left of Bobby. The first person I would call is Paula. I would say, "Hey, what are y'all up to?" She would just say, "What time are you getting here?" We would just laugh. I asked her how she knew, and she said she could hear me driving in the background. After I married B, I stopped going. It placed a damper on my marriage but also on my relationship with the family because they would always ask me when I was going back. For years I didn't return, and I regret that. Paula and I aren't as close as we used to be. Many of my messages or texts go unanswered but not always, thankfully. She still embraces me and accepts me as her sister. I'm usually invited to her family gatherings, especially birthday parties for her kids. Paula also welcomes my son, which I appreciate. Even though things aren't the same, I love her as a sister and will continue to carry on our relationship for as long as possible.

Jodie

Jodie is another one of Bobby's older sisters. She is the silly one, and everyone picks on Jodie. She is always smiling and happy, and she acts silly and crazy. I love her laugh even though it's loud. I always laugh when I hear her laugh. Jodie has always embraced me as a sister as well. We never really got close, but we always had a good time together. We accept each other just as we are. She's still the same crazy

Jodie after all these years, and I love her for it! I also appreciate the fact that Jodie will always respond to my calls or texts. It may be a little late, but she will always respond, and I love that about her.

Angela

I'm closest to his sister, Angela, but it didn't start out that way. Bobby used to tell me she was the sister I had to watch out for. He told me Angela would be the hardest sister to gain acceptance from, and he also used to threaten to get her on me if I ever messed up on him. I laugh now because Angela truly has become a sister to me. I feel so close and connected to her. I always tell her that Bobby would be so proud of how close we are. She always jokingly says that she would have probably given me a hard time had we gotten to meet beforehand. I believe her too! Bobby always used to say, "You mess up, I got four sisters waiting for you!" but Angela was always his go-to. I always used to respond with "I'm not afraid of your sisters!" And I would tell him that his family was going to love me.

Over the years, Angela has been the one who has consistently reached out. She told me that she lost Bobby, but she wasn't losing me. She said, "You better get used to it because you're stuck with me!" I was like, "Well damn" but that's how we are. We always bust each other's chops and pick on each other. She reminds me of Bobby with her competitiveness and that she always has a dang comeback for everything I say! She made it a point to come out and visit me in Hawaii along with her son, her hubby, and of course, Mama. We had a great time and even hiked up the backside of the stairway to heaven, which sucked, but the view at the top was gorgeous. She was mad as hell going up, and I kept saying, "We are almost there, Angela. We're almost there!" On the way down, it was me complaining, and she kept telling me, "We're almost there!" My dumbass wore water shoes because the hike was super last minute; they were all I had at the time. By the end of the hike, she literally helped carry me. If that isn't something Bobby would do, I don't know what is! But she made sure to call me a fatass in the process though! The Pagans always find a way to joke around!

Angela tried to convince me to move out to Texas right when I got out of the army, but I was hesitant. I now had a son, and I didn't know how things were going to be with the family being that so much had changed. She always reassured me that we were family regardless and that my son would also be accepted as family too. I truly appreciate that I can always be open and honest with Angela about my feelings and concerns. She keeps it real, gives it to me straight, but always reassures me in the process. I chose to try to go home to Las Vegas when I got out of the military. But I rang in the year 2018 with the Pagan family in Texas. It was the first time I had seen the family since 2012 and the first time they got to meet my son. It was a good time, and Angela told me that we were always welcomed in Texas. My son adores her. She is his favorite *tia*, and I blame her for converting my son into a Cowboys fan! (Lord, help me!) She has included us in all her plans and even extended an invitation for me and my son to join them on a trip to Puerto Rico, which I gladly accepted. Angela, her hubby, her son, Ana, Bobby's niece, Miguel, his wife, their son, and of course, Mama all took a trip to Puerto Rico. My son and I joined them a day later. It was awesome. I had a wonderful time exploring the island with them.

When I first moved to Texas, Angela opened her home to us. My son and I lived with her until I closed on my house and got to move into the home I have now. She wouldn't let me pay her rent, and she even watched my son for me on Tuesday and Thursday nights when I had to attend my college classes after work. I will forever be grateful to her for opening up her home to us and all that she has done for us.

I finally made the move to Texas. When Bobby and I were together, our plan was to start a family, relocate to Texas, and get his dog Safira back from his mom. I told Mama I would take Safira, but she died before I could do that. I cried when I found out, but I was thankful that I got the chance to meet her and love on her before she died. She was a white pit bull with a brown nose. She was a tough little thing, but she actually let me walk her. He loved that dog. I loved that time with her because once again, she was another physical aspect of Bobby that I had left. I have had my heart set on Texas ever since Bobby passed. I was scared because I had my son, but moving to Texas has been the best decision I've made since I got out. I live right outside of San Antonio, but I still see Angela more than I see anyone else in the Pagan family. I'm close enough to drive down and visit Bobby's gravesite or his family anytime that I want and that is extremely important to me.

Ana

Ana is my age. Our birthdays are literally two days apart, which I always thought was awesome. I felt like I connected well with Ana when I first met the family. She's raw, honest, and always keeps it real. I've always appreciated that about her. When we were preparing for the funeral, I told her I needed an outfit for the funeral. I didn't have very many clothes. Paula and Ana took me to some shop to find something to wear, and I kept grabbing leggings and tried on different tops. I'll never forget when I was in the dressing room, and I heard Ana tell Paula, "Bobby would have said you're dressing for a funeral, not an outfit for the damn club!" I busted up laughing! All I heard her say was, "I said that too loud, way too loud."

When I got out of the dressing room, I just smiled at her, laughed, and told her she was right. I ended up picking out some black slacks and a short sleeve gray top that had what resembled a drooped scarf in the front and had a little black belt around the waist. That's Ana for you though, blunt and honest. I love it and definitely respect her for it! Ana shared her room with me every time I went to visit. I liked that she opened up to me and didn't mind shedding a few tears in front of me. I loved all the stories she would tell me about Bobby and how protective he was of her. I knew the feeling but from a different aspect. Bobby was very protective of me and made it very known that I was his girl. I feel like Ana has a lot of the same features as Bobby, just a much prettier version. Ana is gorgeous! When I was constantly driving down to Texas, we hung out all the time. We even went to 6th Street together to celebrate our birthdays one year. That was fun! I love her so much. Over time, we haven't remained as close as I want to, and I don't get to see her as often. However, she will always be a sister to me. I intend to preserve our relationship for as long as possible.

Chris

Chris is one of Bobby's younger brothers. When I first met Chris, it took a minute for him to warm up to me, but once he did, he was cracking jokes left and right. He was always teasing me about my football team, just like his dang brother! I think Chris looked like a mini version of Bobby with the exception of his hair. Chris has curly hair, and Bobby didn't. I played basketball with him and Miguel at the park one time, and they both seriously kicked my butt in the game. I tried though and kept talking as much crap to them as they were to me; it was a good time. He was a good kid. He just loved to tease me and make fun of me every chance he got. After all those years away when I finally seen Chris, I stopped dead in my tracks. He looked so much like Bobby it was scary. Now that he's older, he really favors Bobby's features. The difference is Chris has a darker skin complexion, he's skinnier, he's shorter, he has curly hair, and Bobby was buffer. (Sorry, bro, but it's true. Better start lifting those weights!) Chris now has two kids, and when I first seen pictures of his daughter, I got sad. She is beautiful and looks a lot like Chris, Bobby, and Ana for that matter. I felt like I had an idea of what my kids might have looked like. Ana doesn't have kids yet, so I only got a glimpse from Chris's kids. His wife, Nohely, was a little standoffish, but she's slowly warming up to me and I've been able to have a couple good conversations with her. When I first moved out here to Texas, Chris was a little standoffish again. After a while, he got back to the same old stuff and started with the jokes and making fun of me for everything, especially with sports. I hardly get to see Chris now, but he's always going to be like a little brother to me, and I always try to bust his chops whenever I do get to see him.

Miguel

Miguel is the youngest of all the siblings. He happens to look a lot like Robert. However, Robert is taller and Miguel is skinny (Robert is really buff), but they look just alike in facial features. Like Chris, Miguel took a minute to warm up to me, but when he finally did, he would tag team with Chris on the jokes. They both would just make fun of the Raiders and throw out a bunch of stats letting me know that "the Raiders are trash." Anything I came up with, they always had a comeback for! Dang Pagan family! They are all competitive, good at spitting out stats, and very quick with the comebacks! I love them for it though. Miguel also has two kids now, and I love his wife, Monica. When I first moved to Texas, she babysat my son for me while I was job searching and continued to care for him up until I moved to San Antonio. Miguel would also cut my son's hair; he is definitely talented. I told him he should look into becoming a barber, but he has other plans. Miguel and I aren't very close, but it's always fun cracking jokes with him anytime he's around. He will always be like a little brother to me, and I love him and his little family to pieces.

I've done many things with the Pagan family. I've attended family barbeques, birthday parties, quinceañeras, holidays, and of course, attended family trips with them. I even had a cake fight with them one time during a family BBQ at a park by some lake here in Texas. My older brother and his friend actually attended that with me, and we all had a good time. I've been to a Texas fair with them, been to the lake, and rode Jet Skis with them, went to a water park with them, and have continued making memories with them. The Pagan family will *always* be my family. I consider them my in-laws even though Bobby and I never had the chance to get married. People don't always understand it, but I say *what is understood never has to be explained.* They are all I have left of Bobby, so I hold each of them near and dear to my heart. They will forever be my family, and I will continue to maintain our relationship for as long as I can regardless of what changes happen in my life over time.

Feeling Alone

To be honest, I am still healing from the loss of my fiancé, and there are many people who just don't understand it. At this point, I don't expect anyone to understand. I will point out that loss is dealt with differently by each person who experiences it. I would also like to point out that no one should tell anyone how to mourn or when they should move on. Quite frankly, I always found it rude and disrespectful when someone told me to move on or asked me why I hadn't gotten over it yet. For future reference, please just don't. Every loss is different. I don't expect my experience or journey to be the same as anyone else, even though we may have similarities. One big difference that sets me apart from most Gold Star Family Members is that I wasn't married to Bobby, so technically, I am not considered a Gold Star Family Member. Granted I went through the same type of loss, but I was only his fiancée, not his wife or blood relative. Therefore, I was very fortunate to have been able to go through each step with his family. I received a Gold Star Family Member pin, but I'm set apart from others, and that is okay. My journey, my experience, and my circumstances have been unique, but God has always had his hand over me. I'd like to offer a word of advice for those in mourning or healing from the loss of a loved one. Never let anyone tell you when they think you should be "over it." Never let anyone tell you that you need to "move on." It is not anyone's place or right to do so regardless of who it is that says it. God is the only one who can heal you from the inside out. God's still working on me. I'm still healing and processing his loss partially because I've clung on to what I have left of Bobby in fear of losing him forever. Partially because the pain has been overwhelming and, at times, unbearable, so I tried to suppress those feelings for years and focus on other things. However, God is persistent in asking me to release that pain and give it all to him. It's a scary thought letting go. Eventually I hope to be in a better place, but that will be in God's perfect timing; no one else has a say so in that.

Being that so much time has passed, I have often felt so alone in trying to express how I feel or even addressing the pain at all. It isn't a comfortable conversation for people, and I get that. Counseling didn't help me at first, maybe because I wasn't ready to open up fully. I am still in therapy and am working through it. I am currently working through different trauma healing techniques such as EMDR and writing. Hopefully with God and my therapy sessions I can eventually get to a place of peace so that I can sleep and function better. My two best friends Rodrigo and Logan have often encouraged me to write about it. I'm not going to lie, I purposely held off for so long because I didn't feel ready to address the pain within me. I didn't feel ready to peel back the Band-Aid I placed over my gushing wound. When I finally started, I had to stop multiple times to weep. I felt the pain as I wrote. While some memories made me smile or laugh, I still cried at the thought of a losing Bobby and the love we shared. To say that writing this book was extremely hard for me is an absolute understatement. I had to hide my emotion from my son, of course, so I mostly wrote this book throughout the wee hours of the night and often wouldn't stop until about six in the morning. The pain that poured out from within me was relentless, I stayed up all night and wept for weeks. While it was extremely difficult to relive the pain and the emotions of everything that had occurred, writing has been the most therapeutic experience for me. I feel like huge weight has been lifted off my chest. However, I am still healing, and it is still very difficult to sleep at night.

Once the house becomes still, my mind starts to race. However, there is something powerful about taking a thought from my mind and writing it down on paper. My thoughts then become something concrete, something I can see with my eyes and hold in my hands. To me, that is not only powerful but also something very beautiful. Memories can fade over time as we age, but when those memories are placed into a picture, letter, or in this case a book, then those memories can live on forever. I recently wrote what I consider to be a poem, if you will. I laid on my bed in the dead of the night, unable to sleep due to my anxiety and my restless thoughts. So I once again took it from my mind and wrote it down to give insight on how I feel when nightfall hits and I'm all alone with my thoughts. I titled it "Who Can I Turn To?"

Who do I talk to when I'm alone at night in pain? Who can I turn to? There is no one that understands it. How can I still be grieving when more than ten years have passed? Sure, I can send a text to his mother or even one of his sisters. Sometimes I'll get a reply. Sometimes I won't depending on the hour of the night. But the hard truth is people no longer want to talk about it, not openly anyway. They only want to remember the happy times they've had with him, and so do I. But unfortunately, that is not my reality. So who can I turn to, to help ease the pain? The answer is simple, no one. I've turned to God, but when it comes to this specific area of my life, my prayers and questions often go unanswered. I know God is looking out for me. He always has, but the pain is still very relevant, still very real. The tears so eloquently run down the cheeks of my face. Soon enough, it is as if a faucet has turned on from deep inside of me, and the tears flow eagerly out of my eyes. The pain of my soul starts to pour out, and I cry as if I were a newborn baby or a young child. So desperately wanting to be held and told that everything is going to be okay. Yet here I am, a grown adult, alone in despair, mourning over the loss of my soul mate. I find myself yearning for him. Yearning to be nestled in the comfort of his arms once again. Tear marks stain my cheeks and drown my pillows. My body quivers, my head hurts, and I cry out for him as quietly as I can in effort not to wake my son who peacefully sleeps in the other room. Sometimes I get so overwhelmed that I have to cry into my pillow to let out the screams of agony. Into my pillow, I let out one bellow at a time at least until the pain begins to resurface and bursts out of me. I desperately weep into my pillow, and as the screams become more frequent, I try to gasp for air to tame my body. At this point, a newborn baby freshly slapped on the bottom by a doctor is nothing in comparison to the screams or cries that I experience deep into the dark of the night. Feelings and expressions can only be ignored or tamed for so long before they force me to face them, and it won't matter if I am ready or not. I can keep myself busy throughout the day, keep my mind focused and in check. But once nightfall hits and it is time to rest, the emotions start to overwhelm me. Like a game of hide-and-seek, ready or not, here they come. My mind starts to race deep into the hours of the night. Rest is forbidden. The unanswered questions start flooding in: *Why Bobby? Why not me instead? Why couldn't we get to spend those last two weeks on leave together if he had to be taken from this earth? Why couldn't I have seen him out there one last time? Why did God take him from me? Why did God want to hurt me so bad? Why do I feel so alone? Why does it hurt so much? Who can I turn to?* No one. I've turned to God over and over, but over time, I have concluded that this pain is mine and mine alone. This grief is mine to bear until my soul learns to heal itself or maybe for the rest of my days. Who really knows? My love for Bobby is eternal.

Shall this pain be eternal as well? I cling to the old saying, "If God brings you to it, He will surely get you through it." I've been told time and time again, God will only give you what you can handle. I often cry out to God, "Lord, I am not as strong as you think I am. I cannot handle this pain. Please, God, take it from me." Dare I question our great Creator? Dare I think that I know what I can and cannot handle? God created me. I am built from strength and resiliency, yet I have buckled to this pain. To help ease it, I try to think of Bobby's laugh or soothing voice, but over the years, it has gotten harder and harder to remember. So finally, I reached out to his sisters. Somebody has to have something, anything with his voice or laugh. Jodie was the first who tried to help, but the video she suggested had no sound. No sound, just like the pain that has been buried deep within me that has been desperately trying to resurface. Stuff it, I say to myself, stuff it so that there is no sound. No hurt, no pain. If only it were that easy. Angela also tried to help, but it upset her as well knowing their collection of videos with his voice or laugh was quite limited, almost extinct, and that hurts. He has become extinct, but I refuse to allow it. My heart, my soul, and my memories will not allow for his extinction—*never*. Ana, my sister, my saving grace, blessed me with a video of Bobby talking and laughing. Oh, how my heart filled with joy, and yet as it played, my body revolted knowing I have lost him. I bawled like a baby while watching it over and over. All those years of stuffing, but I ultimately paid the price for it. Pain and sorrow burst out of me like heat bursts through a kernel of corn. What I would do for one last day with you, my love. What I would do. Your voice, your laugh, your smile all brought so much joy to my heart, and now I yearn for it. I yearn for you, something I can never have again. It hurts so bad to so desperately want something, someone you cannot have. It did not take losing him for me to realize what I had. No, I knew what I had long before. I just never thought I would lose him. Yet being that it must, life has to go on. I have to keep living, so I keep pushing forward as time quickly passes by. I will live on, but I will also carry on his memory for as long as I shall live. His legacy remains and lives on through me, his family, and his friends as each of us carry on beautiful memories of him, pictures of him, and videos of him. It is all we have left of Bobby, and as long as we continue to breathe air and live, he will live on in our hearts and through our wonderful memories. Yet for me that is not enough. No, I need something more definitive, something concrete that can last forever. Who can I turn to? Myself, because God has provided me with the strength and courage I've needed all along. With God anything is possible! By the grace of God I will heal. With God's help I will transfer my thoughts, emotions, and my beautiful memories of Bobby into the pages of a book so that his memory can live on forever.

Conclusion

Bobby showed me a love unlike any other. It is truly difficult to try to explain in words because I feel like nothing I say, truly gives justice to the love nor can adequately describe the love we shared. Bobby taught me what it meant to truly connect with another soul and to love deeply. He showed me what it meant to place another person before yourself. He taught me how to help someone heal when they are hurting, not only to mend the pain but to mend the soul. Bobby taught me to enjoy laughter every chance possible, to enjoy precious moments together, to look deeply into the eyes of another and see beyond the surface, to appreciate a smile and see the beauty in it. He taught me those things by loving me in that way. A way that I had never been loved before. When I cried, Bobby embraced me and forced me to let go of the shame of thinking I was weak, opposite of what I was taught during my childhood. When I was happy, Bobby was overjoyed because he loved to see me smile.

He spent as much time with me as he possibly could during his off time and made such an impact in my life over the course of two years. He knew about my past and didn't judge me for it. Instead he wanted to help me heal. He wanted to show me the love he said I deserved and tried his best to do so. Bobby was amazed by what I experienced during my childhood and the choices I made to rise above everything that was meant to destroy me. He became my biggest supporter, my best friend, my soul mate. He treated me like a queen and promised me that I would always be safe in his arms. Bobby made me feel safe and loved which was new for me. I was able to open up to him about anything and everything without judgment. He would privately let me know when I was in the wrong but remained a gentleman and would always support me regardless. He helped me grow personally and always pushed me to grow professionally as well. He had a lot of patience with me despite my issues and deficits. I am not an easy person to love, and back then, I was still in the process of maturing. I was far from perfect, still am. Yet Bobby loved me for who I was, and nothing ever changed that. He was different, and I loved him for it.

The mere thought of Bobby made me smile and still does to this day. I still get butterflies when I think back on how he made me feel. In the same respect, I still get sad, and the pain is still very real, even though it has been over ten years since I lost him. I truly cherish the memories we shared together. Bobby was everything to me and more. He was my breath of fresh air. He once told me his love for me was stronger than the sun was hot. That he loved me more than the moon had craters. He loved me *more* than the planets are far, and more than the shooting stars are fast. The love we had was rare and beautiful. I have never experienced another love like it, nor have I ever had another connection like I had with Bobby. He was my soul mate and the love of my life. I know we were young, but the love was real, and no one can ever take that from me. Even after death, my love for him has carried on. True love never dies.

I don't visit Bobby's gravesite all the time because it is still hard for me, and I cry every single time that I go. It honestly took me forever to take my son to Bobby's grave. When I finally took him, I explained to him that Bobby was very special to me and that he is now my guardian angel up in heaven. I, of course, always take a bouquet of roses with baby's breath for him. Those are the only flowers that I will ever take him because it is what he brought me the day he gave me the promise ring and asked me to wait for him. I do, however, make it a point to go visit his grave on his birthday, on the anniversary of his death, and on Memorial Day at a minimum. The love I have for Bobby will never diminish nor will it ever die. True love never dies; it lasts forever. He was my soul mate and the absolute love of my life. Onc day, it will be my day to meet our Maker, and I believe in my heart that Bobby will be waiting for me at the pearly gates of heaven. I'm not sure what God has in store for my future, but whatever it is, I am trusting in the process. I'm still alive today, so I know that God is not done using me yet. My life will serve a purpose. Whatever purpose that may be, I know that it will be for the greater good.

To those who are suffering or mourning over the loss of a loved one, please know that you are not alone. People who surround you may not always understand your situation, but there are people out there who understand your pain, myself included. I can't promise it will get any easier, nor can I promise that life will get better. I will say that God has carried me through this far, and I have been able to get through each day, no matter how difficult it was to do so. I still have questions, and there are things that I will never understand, but I rest in the hope that I will see Bobby once again at the gates of heaven. Never feel pressured to move on or get over the loss you face; no one has the right to do that to you. My advice would be to take your time to mourn, embrace the emotion, and find a healthy outlet to let it out, whatever that may be. Cherish the memories that you have of your loved one and find comfort knowing that you can keep their memory alive for as long as you wish. Loss is hard, but life keeps going whether we like it or not. Do what works best for you. Ask God for the strength to face each day even if it is one day at a time, one hour a time, or one moment at a time. There are many of us who struggle to do the same. You got this.

Bobby, until I see you again, I vow to keep your memory alive for as long as I have living breath within me. Our love will never die. True love never dies; it lasts forever. Our love will carry on forever in my heart and in my memories regardless of what changes take place or whoever comes into my life in the future. Shine down on me, Papi, and continue to watch over me, please. Rest in peace, my guardian angel, Specialist Bobby Justin Pagan.

Bobby and I at the Ball

Bobby and I were one of
few couples who weren't
in uniform at the ball.

Bobby and Macias

Bobby driving the impala
(I took this photo)

Bobby in one of his infamous
hats worn backwards and
slightly to the left

Bobby in Afghanistan

One of my favorite photos
of Bobby in Afghanistan

Bobby taking a shot of fireball
right before signing karaoke with
the guys at Burdios' house

Bradley and Bobby

Bobby's head stone along
with the roses I always take
when I visit his grave

4th ID Memorial stone

From left: Logan, me, and
Kortney visiting Bobby's grave

Memorial Stone outside Fort
Carson's main gate where
Bobby's name is displayed

Bobby's casket encasement

I was so out of it I was physically there but mentally I was
struggling to face the fact that I truly lost him forever

Bobby's funeral...watching him be lowered into the ground

In complete shock and trying to process that reality

My S1 team: from rear left SPC Lopez, SGT Krueger,
SPC Contratti, SFC Ocampo, SPC Logan
Middle row from left: SGT Tejeda, CW2
Castenon, CPL Calo, MAJ Fluck, me
Bottom: SGT Wang and SGT Lamping

Afghanistan 2009

Dinner with Scott and Terry

Ángela Pagan and I hiking in Hawaii

From upper left: Jodie, me, Ana, and Paula down in center

My son Cameron, me, and Mama Peggy

SGT Wang and SGT Lamping

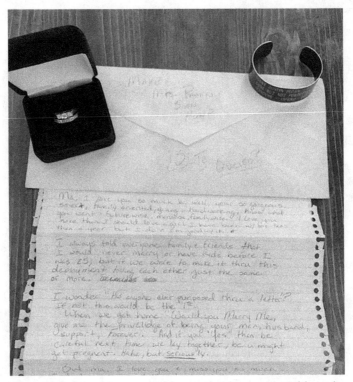

The set of rings, his proposal letter, and his memorial bracelet

Bobby's family at Fort Hood when Robert was being deployed (I took the picture). From left: Richard, Robert, Miguel, Ana, Chris, Mama Peggy, Paula, Angela, and Jodie down in center

Bobby with some of his Brothers and sisters on one of his last visits before deployment. From left: Angela, Miguel, Bobby, Ana, and Chris in front

COL Randy George and SGT Wang about to present me with the Hero of the Month award after COP Keating. SGT Wang was speaking on my behalf and informing everyone why I was receiving the award

CSM Sasser and I catching up on his recent trip to San Antonio

About the Author

Diana Monique Soriano was born and raised in Los Angeles, California, but later moved to Las Vegas, Nevada. After graduating high school, she enlisted in the army and proudly served about ten years of military service. During her deployment in Afghanistan, her life changed forever. Since then, she silently struggled with PTSD, mourning the loss of her fiancé, proving herself as a female soldier, and finding herself again after rising through adversity. Diana was honorably discharged as a staff sergeant in the United States Army. She wanted to share her experiences in hopes of positively impacting the lives of others through her story, to encourage others and inform them that they are not alone in their struggles. She is now an army civilian living in Texas and has earned three college degrees, including a master's in human resources. Diana is determined to overcome all obstacles she encounters in order to pave the way of success and leave a legacy for her son to carry on.

CPSIA information can be obtained
at www.ICGtesting.com
Printed in the USA
BVHW080049180122
626430BV00001B/94

9 781098 091613